WORLD COLOR-PICTURE ALBUM

WORLD COLOR-PICTURE ALBUM

Text by Paul S. Newman

WORLD PUBLISHING
TIMES MIRROR
NEW YORK

Published by The World Publishing Company
110 East 59th Street, New York, N.Y. 10022
Published simultaneously in Canada
by Nelson, Foster & Scott Ltd.

First printing—1972

Copyright © 1972 by The World Publishing Company
Library of Congress catalog card number: 72-79859
ISBN 0-529-04938-4 (trade edition)
0-529-04939-2 (library edition)
Printed in the United States of America

WORLD PUBLISHING
TIMES MIRROR

CONTENTS

Once the automobile gas engine had been invented, man's ancient dream of powered flight was possible. Men had risen into the air in balloons and gliders, but on December 17th, 1903, when Orville Wright flew his plane off the ground, it was the first powered flight of a heavier-than-air machine. The Wright brothers' plane flew 120 feet and was airborne for just twelve seconds.

The army ordered its first aircraft from the Wright brothers in 1908. Until 1911, the army, which then also served as our air force, had only one pilot to fly its lone plane which was able to pursue an enemy at just over 40 miles an hour.

When the United States entered World War I in 1917, the army had only some 55 planes. Most Americans flew in foreign planes like the French Spad during the war and were credited with shooting down over 700 enemy planes and 80 balloons.

Aircraft design and development moved quickly, and by 1912 a plane flew over 100 miles an hour. In 1962 the experimental X-15 rocket plane hit more than 4,000 miles an hour!

An army pilot flying a Curtiss "Jenny" began the first regularly scheduled airmail deliveries in America.

It was in a German Fokker T-2 that two Americans made the first crossing of the United States without a single stop.

In a plane less than 28 feet long, Charles Lindbergh became the first man to fly across the Atlantic Ocean alone, making the trip from New York to Paris in 33 hours and 30 minutes.

The De Havilland "Comet" was among the earliest jet planes used for carrying passengers. It was the forerunner of the huge Boeing 747, which carries about 400 people.

The autogiro (unlike the helicopter which it seems to resemble) has a front propeller which makes it fly. The rotor on top is not turned by an engine but by air pressure. To take off, the autogiro first has to taxi on the ground, while a helicopter can lift straight up into the air.

Recent developments suggest that the aircraft of the future will be able to fly higher, faster, and land in less space.

WRIGHT BROTHERS' AIRPLANE 1903

CURTISS HYDROPLANE 1911

SPAD 1917

CURTISS JN-4D "JENNY" 1917

CURTISS NC4 1919

AUTOGIRO 1923

FOKKER T2 1923

AIRCRAFT

FORD TRIMOTOR 1924

SIKORSKY HELICOPTER S-64 1962

RYAN "SPIRIT OF ST. LOUIS" 1927

BOEING 247 1933

DOUGLAS DC3 1935

BOEING B17E 1941

DOUGLAS DC4-5-6-7 SERIES 1942-53

BOEING B47 1947

DE HAVILLAND "COMET" 1952

BOEING 747 1966

CONCORDE 1970

HAWKER "HARRIER" P1127 VTOL 1962

Anatomy is the study of man's body.

Since ancient people regarded the human body as sacred, they did not dissect, or cut up, a dead person's body. Not until dissection was permitted was man really able to learn about himself. In the fourteenth century dissection was permitted as part of the study of medicine.

The first great book on anatomy was published in 1543, written by Andreas Vesalius. In 1628 the English doctor William Harvey published a book explaining how the blood circulated in the human body.

Two main systems of "tubes," or blood vessels, carry the blood to and from the heart. Blood leaving the heart goes through the lungs where it gets oxygen, which it carries around the body and then returns for a fresh supply.

The arteries carry the blood from the heart.

Tiny blood vessels called capillaries carry the blood between the arteries and the veins.

The veins return the blood to the heart.

If an artery is cut, the blood spurts out in the same rhythm as the heart is pumping. If a vein is cut, the blood flows steadily and slowly.

Blood flows through some arteries at the speed of twenty inches a second, while in some veins it travels at six inches a second.

In the course of seventy years, the heart beats about 2,600,000,000 times and pumps 150,000 tons of blood.

The heart is basically a muscle used for pumping blood through the body's 100,000 miles of blood vessels.

The right side of the heart pumps blood into the lungs, while the left side pumps the blood from the lungs through the whole body. In about a minute, five quarts of blood circulate through the body.

The brain is the finest computer ever designed, receiving its input from our senses so we are aware of what is happening around us.

The brain sends out messages to our body and controls such things as our feeling hunger or even feeling anger.

An adult's brain weighs about five pounds. But a brain's weight does not have anything to do with intelligence or the smartest creature would be the elephant with its eleven-pound brain.

ANATOMY

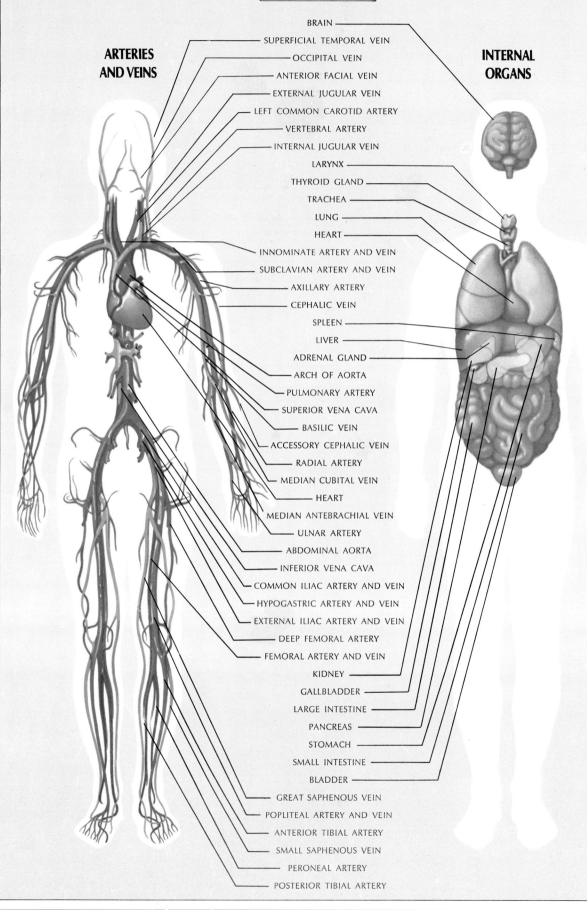

ARTERIES AND VEINS

INTERNAL ORGANS

BRAIN
SUPERFICIAL TEMPORAL VEIN
OCCIPITAL VEIN
ANTERIOR FACIAL VEIN
EXTERNAL JUGULAR VEIN
LEFT COMMON CAROTID ARTERY
VERTEBRAL ARTERY
INTERNAL JUGULAR VEIN
LARYNX
THYROID GLAND
TRACHEA
LUNG
HEART
INNOMINATE ARTERY AND VEIN
SUBCLAVIAN ARTERY AND VEIN
AXILLARY ARTERY
CEPHALIC VEIN
SPLEEN
LIVER
ADRENAL GLAND
ARCH OF AORTA
PULMONARY ARTERY
SUPERIOR VENA CAVA
BASILIC VEIN
ACCESSORY CEPHALIC VEIN
RADIAL ARTERY
MEDIAN CUBITAL VEIN
HEART
MEDIAN ANTEBRACHIAL VEIN
ULNAR ARTERY
ABDOMINAL AORTA
INFERIOR VENA CAVA
COMMON ILIAC ARTERY AND VEIN
HYPOGASTRIC ARTERY AND VEIN
EXTERNAL ILIAC ARTERY AND VEIN
DEEP FEMORAL ARTERY
FEMORAL ARTERY AND VEIN
KIDNEY
GALLBLADDER
LARGE INTESTINE
PANCREAS
STOMACH
SMALL INTESTINE
BLADDER
GREAT SAPHENOUS VEIN
POPLITEAL ARTERY AND VEIN
ANTERIOR TIBIAL ARTERY
SMALL SAPHENOUS VEIN
PERONEAL ARTERY
POSTERIOR TIBIAL ARTERY

The atmosphere is a gaseous covering which surrounds our earth. It contains the air we breathe.

Our air is made up of gases, water vapor and solid particles like dust. The two most common gases in our air are nitrogen, which represents 78% of the gases in air and oxygen, which represents 21%. About a dozen other gases make up the remaining 1%. Of those minor gases, argon is the most important.

The sky above us in the day seems blue, because the air particles in our atmosphere are not transparent and they reflect and scatter sunlight in a way which gives us a bluish light.

Extending from the earth's surface to about five miles above the poles and ten miles above the equator is the troposphere. We live in the troposphere, and our weather is made there.

Above it is the cold stratosphere, where the temperature of the lowest layer is 70 degrees below zero.

From fifty miles above the earth and extending up to 300 miles is the ionosphere. Its name comes from the "ions" that fill this layer of the atmosphere. Ions are tiny, electrified molecules or atoms. Because radio signals can be bounced off the ionosphere, we can radio around the world.

The atmosphere has weight and is heaviest near the earth's surface. The higher you go, the less oxygen there is, which is why climbers on very high mountains take oxygen tanks and why cabins in jet planes have air pumped into them to make breathing easier for passengers.

On the way to the moon, man has broken out of the earth's atmosphere and gone into airless space.

From the surface of the earth to its middle is about 4,000 miles. The outside of the earth is its soil. Most of the world's 57,230,000 square miles of land surface are covered by soil.

The upper layer, or topsoil, is where we grow our food. In colonial times, America's topsoil was nine inches deep. Today it averages only six inches in depth. But chemical fertilizers and the planting of special crops can help preserve and increase the remaining topsoil. Its greatest natural enemies are too much rain and wind.

Below the topsoil are two other layers, or "horizons," where new topsoil is slowly forming.

ATMOSPHERIC LAYERS AND SOIL LAYERS
MAN'S PENETRATION OF THE ATMOSPHERE

A. 1903 – Wright Brothers' first flight.

B. 1936 – DC-3 – Commercial air transport cruises at 10,000-12,000 ft.

C. Oct. 1947 – Bell X-1 – First jet to break the sound barrier, 12,000 ft.

D. May 4, 1961 – Highest manned balloon, 21.5 miles.

E. Oct. 1957 – Sputnik – First man-made satellite, 600 miles.

F. 1961 – Mercury – First manned suborbital rocket, 116 miles.

G. Aug. 22, 1963 – X-15 – Highest manned jet flight, 67 miles.

H. July 21, 1969 – Apollo – Man lands on the moon, 238,857 miles.

Since it was invented near the end of the 1800's, the gas-powered automobile has spread around the world until today there are over 100 million cars on the road with more than half of these in the United States.

The first known self-propelled "car" was a three-wheeled steam-driven carriage built by Nicolas Cugnot about 1770. It went two and one-half miles an hour but had to stop about every 100 feet to build up more steam.

As more steam-powered horseless carriages appeared in the 1800's, England passed the Red Flag law requiring someone to walk ahead of the horseless carriage with a red flag by day and a red lantern by night to warn oncoming drivers of horse-drawn carriages. Toll roads and bridges began charging so much more for horseless carriages that they became too costly to operate in England.

There is no agreement as to who first invented the gas-powered car, but the first such car to be driven in the United States was built by the Duryea brothers in 1893.

The Cadillac was the first car to have interchangeable parts with other Cadillacs, so they could easily be replaced.

Henry Ford was the man who really began to mass produce cars. The frame of his car was pulled between two rows of workers, who added parts as the frame passed their station. The Model T was assembled in about two hours.

Many early cars were luxury cars, with the famed "Silver Ghost" selling for over $20,000.

One thing that kept most women from driving the first cars was the need to start them by laboriously turning a hand crank. Charles Kettering's electric self-starter solved this around 1912 and put women behind the wheel.

Cars have changed our way of life. They have given us the freedom to travel easily; let families move from the city to the suburb, from where a parent could commute to work; and caused the building of improved roads. But the car has also caused such problems as air pollution.

How important the auto is to the American economy can be judged by the fact that directly or indirectly, over 10,000,000 people in the United States work in this industry.

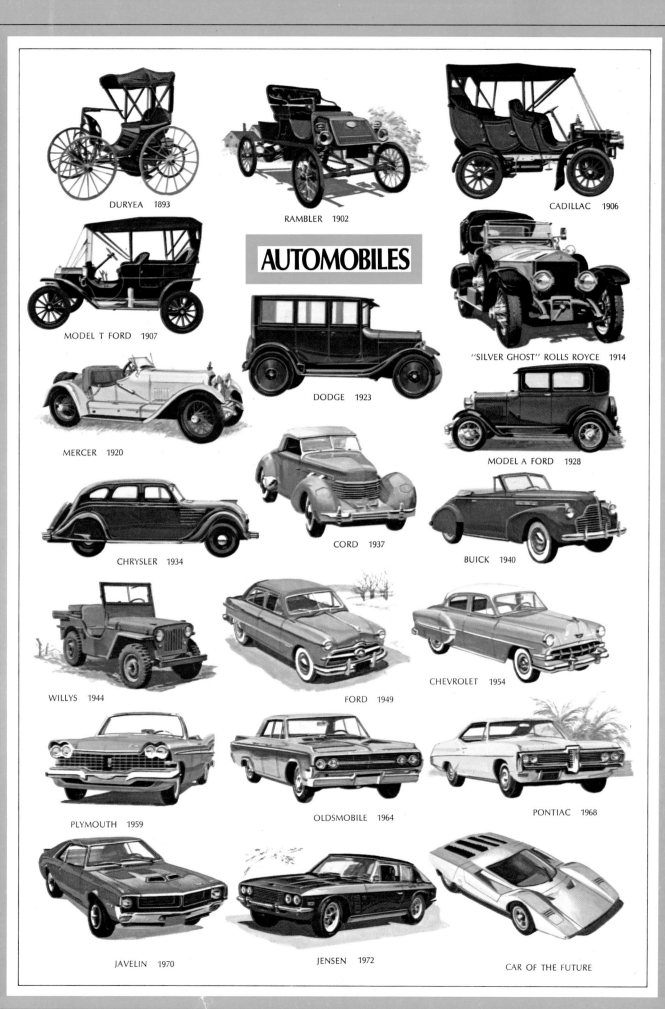

DURYEA 1893

RAMBLER 1902

CADILLAC 1906

AUTOMOBILES

MODEL T FORD 1907

DODGE 1923

"SILVER GHOST" ROLLS ROYCE 1914

MERCER 1920

CORD 1937

MODEL A FORD 1928

CHRYSLER 1934

BUICK 1940

WILLYS 1944

FORD 1949

CHEVROLET 1954

PLYMOUTH 1959

OLDSMOBILE 1964

PONTIAC 1968

JAVELIN 1970

JENSEN 1972

CAR OF THE FUTURE

Tropical birds are remarkable for their brilliant colors. These colors probably serve a protective purpose, helping them blend into the colorful jungle where most of them live. There are more kinds of birds in the tropics than anywhere in the world.

Except for the flamingo, the frigate bird, some types of ibis and a few others, none of these birds are found in North America.

The bird of paradise, one of the most beautiful of all, when first seen in the South Pacific was called the bird of the sun, for it was supposed to live all its life in the air, following the sun and only landing when it died.

The cassowary of Australia and the island of New Guinea can kill a man with one kick from its sharp-clawed leg.

When the South American hoatzin is born, it has claws on its wings. Since it cannot fly up to a tree branch soon after hatching, it climbs up by means of the wing claws.

The Mexican jacana's unusually long toes and claws spread out its weight so well that it can run across the water on large plant leaves.

The macaw is one of the longest-living birds, having been known to live for over sixty years.

While the ostrich cannot fly and has only two toes on each foot, it is the swiftest runner of all the birds, reaching up to fifty miles an hour in a short spurt.

The sociable weaver lives under a huge common nest roof in South Africa. This community roof is often the size of an African hut's roof and almost 100 separate nests have been counted under a single grass-and-stick roof.

The sacred ibis was the holy bird of ancient Egypt. It arrived in summer, and as the Nile River got lower in the fall, it departed. The ibis is found in several types in the United States, but unlike the heron, which it resembles, the ibis keeps its neck stretched out when it flies.

Among tropical birds, as among nearly all birds, the male is usually more colorful than the female.

TROPICAL BIRDS

Water birds live on the water or by it. They include the shorebirds who run along our sandy beaches like the plover; birds that swim on lakes like the grebe; birds of the swamps like the coot and rail; birds of our coastal waters such as the pelican and cormorant, and those who range far out on the ocean like the albatross.

Some water birds live only in fresh water, but many ducks, terns and gulls live in both fresh and salt water.

While the penguin is unable to fly at all, the albatross can keep aloft, gliding on wind currents over the ocean for several days without coming down to rest.

Reaching almost twelve feet from the end of one wing to the end of the other, the wandering albatross has the greatest wingspread of any bird.

A water bird migrates, or travels from its winter home to its summer nesting site, further than any other type bird. Every year the arctic tern flies a 22,000-mile round trip from its winter home in the Antarctic to where it lays its eggs in the Arctic Circle.

The courting habits of water birds vary greatly. Storks wind their necks around each other as if embracing. The male penguin drops a pebble in front of the female of his choice.

The bills of water birds come in many shapes, from the funny looking spoonbill's flattened one to the puffin's colorful big bill and the curlew's graceful, down-turned one.

Some water birds, such as the mallard duck, are surface feeders, poking their bills just below the surface. Others are divers and the loon can plunge over 150 feet underwater.

When diving for fish, a cormorant can remain underwater a considerable time. In the Orient, fishermen fasten a collar around the neck of a cormorant and use it to fish for them. The bird has to surface to be able to swallow, but the collar keeps it from eating its catch.

Sailors named the booby because of its seemingly stupid way of landing on a ship and letting itself be caught for food without trying to defend itself with its sharp beak.

The stormy petral gained its name because sailors thought seeing one out at sea meant that a storm was approaching. It is also called Mother Carey's chicken. That name came from a slurring of the Latin *Mater Cara,* which means the Blessed Virgin Mary. When flying close to the ocean, it often pats the water with its legs and seems to be "walking" on the surface.

WATER BIRDS

Ever since man first floated on a single log across the water, he has been building boats and ships.

The Egyptians were among the earliest to construct large ships which were steered by one or more paddles and a handle that turned them, the tiller.

The trireme solved the problem of giving a ship more speed without making it longer, by simply stacking more rowers above each other. Some triremes had almost two hundred rowers, and, because they could turn quickly, used their beak, or bow, as a weapon.

The Roman merchant ships depended on sail to bring them grain from Egypt in vessels over 180 feet long. St. Paul was shipwrecked on a typical Roman merchant ship carrying 267 people.

The fierce Viking raiding ships were oared by 30 to 64 rowers.

It was in the caravel that the Spanish and Portuguese explorers first ventured into the Atlantic.

Probably the greatest assemblage of Venetian galleys was at the battle of Lepanto in 1571, when Venice used 208 galleys.

Warships became larger and better armed during the next 200 years and Nelson's "Victory" was 186 feet long, had 100 guns, and a crew of over 500.

Americans designed the sleek and speedy clipper ships. Because immigrants had to provide their own food when they left Europe for America, its rapid crossing made the clipper ship their favored transport.

Fulton made the first practical use of steam, and his paddlewheeler commuted between New York City and Albany on the Hudson. He advised passengers that "a shelf has been added to each berth, on which gentlemen will please put their boots, shoes and clothes, that the cabin will not be encumbered."

Giant luxury liners like the 1,000-foot Queen Mary offered their travelers everything from a movie theater to an indoor squash court.

But even now, steam power is giving way to atomic power. And the boat of the future is the hydrofoil, which is already in use in a small version. As it gathers speed, the hydrofoil skims above the water, and because it does not have to push through the water, it can reach speeds over sixty miles an hour.

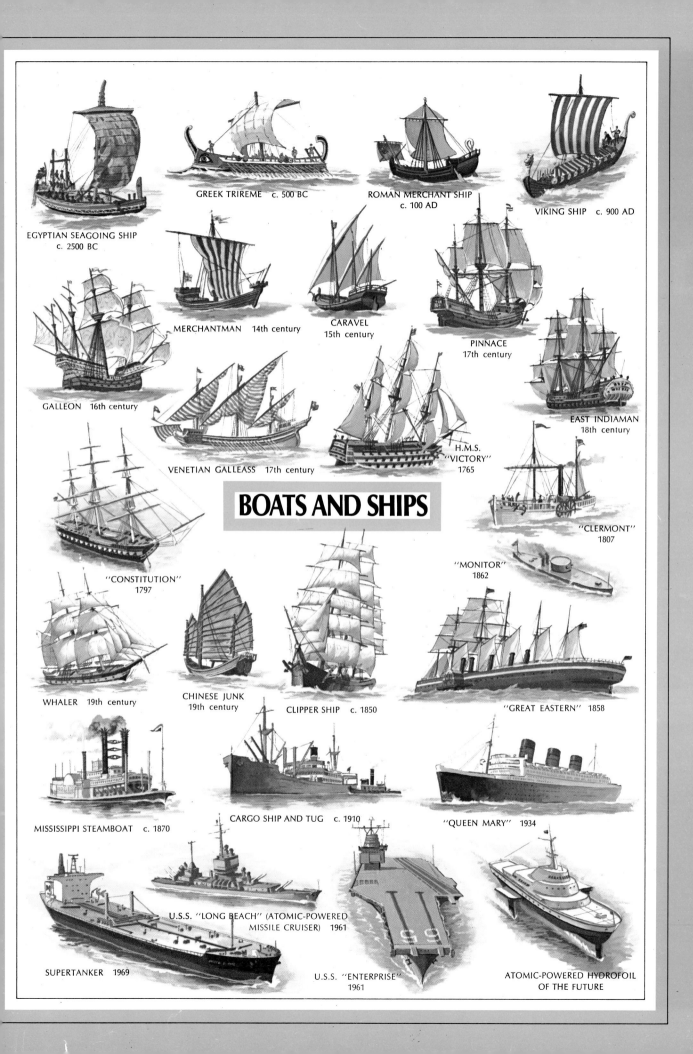

EGYPTIAN SEAGOING SHIP
c. 2500 BC

GREEK TRIREME   c. 500 BC

ROMAN MERCHANT SHIP
c. 100 AD

VIKING SHIP   c. 900 AD

MERCHANTMAN   14th century

CARAVEL
15th century

PINNACE
17th century

GALLEON   16th century

EAST INDIAMAN
18th century

VENETIAN GALLEASS   17th century

H.M.S.
"VICTORY"
1765

BOATS AND SHIPS

"CLERMONT"
1807

"CONSTITUTION"
1797

"MONITOR"
1862

WHALER   19th century

CHINESE JUNK
19th century

CLIPPER SHIP   c. 1850

"GREAT EASTERN"   1858

MISSISSIPPI STEAMBOAT   c. 1870

CARGO SHIP AND TUG   c. 1910

"QUEEN MARY"   1934

SUPERTANKER   1969

U.S.S. "LONG BEACH" (ATOMIC-POWERED
MISSILE CRUISER)   1961

U.S.S. "ENTERPRISE"
1961

ATOMIC-POWERED HYDROFOIL
OF THE FUTURE

Over the centuries man has changed the style of his buildings as much as the style of his clothes.

The use of a building often determined its form. A Gothic cathedral had to serve a different purpose from the fortress-like palace of the Strozzi family.

Building material has changed from the sun-dried bricks of the early Egyptians to the marble of the Greeks to the stone work of the Middle Ages and to the glass, steel and poured concrete of our time. Often the material itself limited the form of a building. Steel allows modern builders to put up skyscrapers. Poured concrete permits buildings to have strange shapes.

The top of the Great Pyramid of Egypt reaches to about the fortieth floor of a present-day building. For some twenty years, over 100,000 slaves worked to make this tomb for the ruler, or Pharoah, Khufu.

The Parthenon was a Greek temple built to honor Athena, the goddess and protector of Athens. With its pleasing dimensions and Doric columns, it is probably the finest example of classic architecture. It was begun in 447 B.C. Some two thousand years later, the Turks stored gunpowder inside it. During an attack, an artillery shell exploded the gunpowder, which blew out the walls and damaged much of the 228-foot-long shrine.

Westminster Abbey has been the site of the crowning of all English rulers from William the Conqueror to Queen Elizabeth II with the exception of Edward V. Begun under King Edward the Confessor in 1050, the Abbey's western towers were not completed until 1740.

Mayan temples were made of stone steps which led to an altar at the top, where the priests led the religious services.

Because they learned how to use a pointed instead of a rounded arch, the builders of Gothic cathedrals were able to raise magnificent stone towers high in the air. Stained-glass windows gave the buildings a lighter feeling.

St. Basil's Church in Moscow, with its twisted domes and brilliantly colored walls, shows the influence of Byzantine architecture from the Middle East.

Just as our taste in clothes changes so does our taste in architecture. The Astrodome and the Trade Towers, which look very modern today, will probably look old-fashioned to our grandchildren.

BUILDINGS AND PEOPLE

GREAT PYRAMID, EGYPT   2500 BC

PARTHENON, ATHENS
400 BC

MAYAN TEMPLE, YUCATÁN   1000 AD

TEMPLE OF HEAVEN, PEKING
MING DYNASTY

ST. BASIL'S, MOSCOW   16th CENTURY

GOTHIC CATHEDRAL
REIMS 13th CENTURY

WESTMINSTER ABBEY
LONDON   11th CENTURY

TAJ MAHAL, AGRA   17th CENTURY

PALAZZO STROZZI
FLORENCE   15th CENTURY

ALCAZAR, SEGOVIA   15th CENTURY

AIR FORCE CHAPEL
COLORADO SPRINGS   1962

JOHNSON GLASS HOUSE
NEW CANAAN, CONN. 1949

GUGGENHEIM MUSEUM, N.Y.C.   1959

ASTRODOME, HOUSTON   1965

TRADE TOWERS, N.Y.C.   1972

A caterpillar is the second stage in the life of a butterfly. After the egg hatches, a small caterpillar comes out.

Like an accordian, the caterpillar keeps expanding and growing out of its own skin. It has six eyes on each side of its head. Its strong jaws and sharp teeth chew up millions of dollars worth of food crops yearly.

Some caterpillars are protected by needle-like hairs that stick an attacker. Others have poison spines which give a powerful sting.

When the caterpillar reaches its full size, it attaches itself to a leaf or twig on a branch and spins a silk-like cocoon about itself. Out of this comes the beautiful butterfly.

While caterpillars destroy crops, the butterfly helps flowers grow. It does this by bringing pollen from one flower to another as it stops to drink nectar. The mixing of the pollen causes fruit and seeds to grow on the plant.

Once a butterfly is born, it does not grow. Butterflies range in size from less than an inch to the Victoria, which is nine inches from wing tip to wing tip. The biggest North American butterfly is the tiger swallowtail with its five-inch wingspread.

Unlike the caterpillar, the butterfly has no teeth. For protection it depends on its coloration to hide itself among leaves and flowers. The monarch butterfly, however, has an unpleasant taste which keeps birds from eating it.

In winter, some butterflies travel to warmer parts of the country. Great masses of monarch butterflies gather in the northern states in the fall and fly to the Gulf states. Then, in spring, many of them return north.

The painted lady butterfly commutes all the way from the west coast to Hawaii, flying over the ocean, while the mourning cloak hibernates, going to "sleep" in some sheltered place.

The more than 90,000 known types of butterflies can be distinguished from moths in several ways. The antennae of butterflies end in a knob while those of moths are hairy. Most butterflies have slender bodies, and most moths have chunky bodies. When not flying, a butterfly folds its wings upright above its back, but the moth rests with its wings stretched out flat.

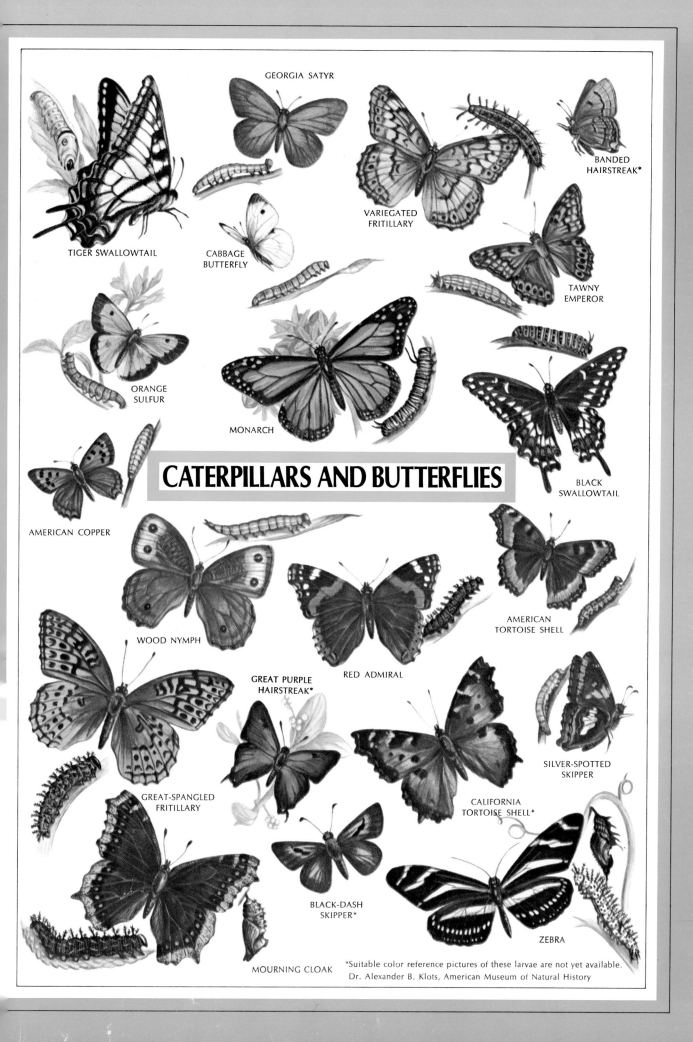

GEORGIA SATYR

BANDED
HAIRSTREAK*

VARIEGATED
FRITILLARY

TIGER SWALLOWTAIL

CABBAGE
BUTTERFLY

TAWNY
EMPEROR

ORANGE
SULFUR

MONARCH

BLACK
SWALLOWTAIL

CATERPILLARS AND BUTTERFLIES

AMERICAN COPPER

AMERICAN
TORTOISE SHELL

WOOD NYMPH

GREAT PURPLE
HAIRSTREAK*

RED ADMIRAL

SILVER-SPOTTED
SKIPPER

GREAT-SPANGLED
FRITILLARY

CALIFORNIA
TORTOISE SHELL*

BLACK-DASH
SKIPPER*

ZEBRA

MOURNING CLOAK

*Suitable color reference pictures of these larvae are not yet available.
Dr. Alexander B. Klots, American Museum of Natural History

Both wild and domestic cats belong to the same animal family. All cats are hunters, feeding on meat which they tear apart with their claws.

Cats are armed with claws at the end of each toe. Most cats can completely cover their claws inside a paw sheathe when their paws are relaxed. They shed their claws several times yearly.

While cats can see better than a human in the dark, they cannot see in total darkness. The iris, or colored part around the pupil of a cat's eye, narrows in bright light and widens in the dark to admit more light. Cats' eyes shine at night because light is reflected by part of their inner eye.

Unlike other mammals, cats have two sets of vocal cords, which is why wild cats can make such varied calls.

The lion is the largest, with the male lion measuring almost ten feet from the tip of his nose to the end of his tail. Only the male has a mane. When attacked, the smaller female is the more dangerous. A lion can leap over twenty feet.

The jaguar, found in South America, often becomes a man-eater.

The male leopard weighs over 100 pounds, and he is so strong that he can haul a dead prey weighing 150 pounds up onto a tree branch well above the ground.

The lynx is the only wild cat with tufted ear tips. Thanks to its wide feet, it can easily walk on the snow.

No animal can outrun a cheetah in a short dash, because it can race at 65 miles an hour.

Cats were probably first domesticated by the Egyptians, who used them to get rid of rats and mice from their grain storage rooms. The Egyptians prized the domestic cat so highly that punishment for killing a cat was usually death. When a pet cat died, its owner shaved his own eyebrows as a sign of mourning.

Phoenician traders from the Middle East may have introduced the domestic cat into Europe about 1000 B.C.

The domestic short-haired probably descended from the African wildcat and was the first cat that man tamed.

The true Manx is the only tailless cat.

The Persian is a very rare breed and has a fluffy hair collar called a ruff, as does the Angora.

Most domestic cats live about fourteen years.

CATS

WILD

BAY LYNX

CANADA LYNX

CARACAL

CHEETAH

COUGAR

JAGUARUNDI

JAGUAR

LEOPARD

SERVAL

LION

OCELOT

MARGAY

CLAW

sheathed   exposed

in dark   EYE   in light

SNOW LEOPARD

TIGER

DOMESTIC

CHINCHILLA

MANX

PERSIAN

ANGORA

SIAMESE

DOMESTIC SHORTHAIRED

Coelenterates are soft-bodied animals, most of whom live in the ocean. There are about 9,000 different coelenterates, and among them are the simplest forms of life. Only the protozoa and sponge have simpler bodies. The coelenterate gets its name from the large digestive cavity which makes up most of its body.

Some coelenterates swim about freely like the jellyfish, while others are fixed to the sea bottom at one end like the sea anemone.

Corals often form huge colonies, as new corals attach themselves to the skeletons of the dead ones. In time, the coral mass grows large enough to form an underwater reef. Corals come in many forms, including the lace-like sea fan.

The Great Barrier Reef of Australia runs for over a thousand miles along that continent's coast, all formed by one coral attaching itself to another and leaving behind its limestone skeleton.

Corals do not form colonies merely in clusters or lines; sometimes they form a circle and inside this ring of coral there is an ocean lagoon. This coral formation is called an atoll. Many islands in the South Pacific are coral atolls.

Underwater coral is dangerous because it can cut a swimmer, and if the coral is alive it may cause the wound to become infected, which is why swimmers are advised to look and admire coral, but not to touch it.

The sea pens get their name because they resemble the old quill pens. They grow to over a foot in length and are found in both the Atlantic and Pacific oceans. When the water around them is disturbed, their feathery part is pulled in flat against the stem and they seem to vanish.

Shaped like an open umbrella, the jellyfish gets its name from the soft, jelly-like mass inside its body. The jellyfish swims by expanding its body and then squeezing out the water. Around the mouth of most jellyfish are tentacles which have stinging cells. These explode on contact with a foreign body, shooting out poisoned barbs or hairs which can paralyze the victim. The eight-inch-long Portugese man-of-war, which floats on the surface of the ocean, has hundred-foot-long tentacles which can give a person a dangerous sting.

Hydras are born by two methods. They can form as a bud on their parents' bodies, breaking off later to go away on their own, or they can hatch from eggs.

Some coelenterates are found growing on the sea bottom at a depth of over 15,000 feet. Sea anemones have been known to live over seventy years.

PORTUGUESE MAN-OF-WAR

BROWN HYDRA

SEA NETTLE

STONY CORAL (Close-up)

TUBE ANEMONE

MILLEPORE

SIPHONOPHORE "By-the-wind sailor"

(detail) SHEATHED HYDROID

STALKED JELLYFISH

SEA FAN

SOFT CORAL

PLUMOSE ANEMONE

BLUE CORAL

Blue Inside

COELENTERATES

FEATHER HYDROID

GIANT JELLYFISH

AGGREGATED ANEMONE

SEA PEN

SOLITARY POLYP

SEA PEN

DAHLIA ANEMONE

COMMON JELLYFISH

SEA FAN

STAGHORN CORAL

MOON JELLYFISH

SEA WHIP

GREEN HYDRA

ORGAN-PIPE CORAL

CLUB-HEADED HYDROID

CORONATE JELLYFISH

BRAIN CORAL

Crustaceans are a group of animals which include such shellfish as the lobster, shrimp and crab, as well as land creatures like the woodlice.

Most of the thousands of crustaceans have a protective shell. The more lime the shell contains, the harder the shell.

Generally, crustaceans are found in the water and have jointed legs. The legs of one ocean crustacean are five feet long.

Most crustaceans shed their shells, slipping out of the shell while a new and larger one is forming on their bodies.

As the crustacean pulls out of its shell, it often loses a leg or a feeler. If it grows back, the new part is usually smaller than the original one, which is why so many lobsters have uneven claws.

The North American lobster lives close to the shore in the summer, and seeks deeper water for the winter. It takes the lobster about five years to grow big enough to be worth catching for food.

The hermit crab is a continual house-hunter, living in the shells others have left. When the hermit crab is small, it settles in old shells of periwinkles or mudsnails. When larger, it seeks the moonshell and welk's shell.

The green crab belongs to the group called swimming crabs. This group is distinguished by having the end of their back legs somewhat flattened. The flattened surface on their back legs serves as paddles, helping them swim as they hunt for food.

Spider crabs are marked by their unusually long legs. They are found in beds of floating kelp or in pools of ocean water left when the tide goes out. If bothered, they will nip a person.

When a female crab lays her eggs, they stick to her body until they hatch into larvae. But the larvae do not look at all like a crab.

The male fiddler crab has one huge claw, which he uses for fighting other males over a mate. Fiddler crabs live in burrows under the beach.

Barnacles are built like shrimps, but differ from most crustaceans in their growth process. Their eggs hatch into free-swimming larvae, which feed and change shape as they grow. Then they attach themselves to a rock, wood or a wooden ship's hull for their "rest period." During this time, the barnacle grows its shell.

Perhaps the oddest thing about a crustacean is its eye at the end of a stalk. Their eyes can look all around. But if the eye stalk breaks off, instead of a new eye growing back, it is replaced with a "feeler," or tentacle.

BURROWING CRAYFISH

NORWEGIAN LOBSTER

CORAL SHRIMP

LAND CRAB

SPIDER CRAB

SPINY LOBSTER

GOOSE BARNACLE

CAVE CRAYFISH

PRAWN

RED KRILL

POND CRAYFISH

GREEN CRAB

FAIRY SHRIMP

FIDDLER CRAB

CRUSTACEANS

BRINE SHRIMP

SOW BUG

ACORN BARNACLE

LOCUST LOBSTER

WATER FLEA

COMMON COMMERCIAL SHRIMP

FRESHWATER OSTRACOD

MARINE COPEPOD

OPOSSUM SHRIMP

rolled up

BEACH FLEA

PILL BUG

NORTH AMERICAN LOBSTER

STOMATOPOD (Mantis Shrimp)

STALKED BARNACLE

HERMIT CRAB

GRIBBLE

The egg not only contains the unborn young bird or reptile, but also holds the food it needs to grow, and it is covered by a protective shell.

It is not the yolk, but a germ-spot, or nucleus, on the yolk that finally becomes the young.

Birds' eggs vary in size from the ostrich's three-pound egg that is six inches long to the hummingbird's egg of less than half an inch which weighs two hundredths of an ounce.

While the hornbill lays only one egg a year, the domestic duck lays about 350.

The color of eggs varies widely. It is believed the reason for their color and markings is to enable them to blend in with the nest or background so that egg-eating animals cannot find them too easily.

Bird eggs come in many shapes. While most are shaped like the ordinary breakfast egg laid by a hen, the plover's egg looks like a pear and the screech owl's egg is round.

Birds lay their eggs in countless places—in nests, on bare rocks, below the ground in burrows, inside trees, and on mud platforms.

To hatch, the eggs must be kept warm. Usually the female sits on the eggs, but the male phalarope is the egg-sitter in that family. While a sparrow's egg takes only twelve days to hatch, some penguin eggs do not hatch before sixty days.

Reptile eggs, in addition to being hard-shelled like bird eggs, are sometimes soft-shelled.

While an African tortoise lays only one egg a year, some sea turtles lay over 200, and the python snake lays almost 200 eggs.

Most reptiles bury their eggs and then leave them to hatch on their own. The boa snake guards its eggs, coiling its powerful body around them where they lay on the ground.

In some reptiles, however, the eggs hatch inside the mother and the young seem to be born alive, as in mammals like dogs and cats, rather than hatched from eggs.

Because most reptiles leave their eggs after laying them and are not there to help their young when they break out of the egg, reptile eggs contain enough food so that the young will grow big enough to be independent by the time they hatch.

AMERICAN GOLDEN PLOVER

BROWN THRASHER

MUTE SWAN

CARDINAL

COMMON GULL

WHIPPOORWILL

NIGHTINGALE

RING-NECKED PHEASANT

KINGBIRD

BLACK-CAPPED
CHICKADEE

CARRION CROW

EASTERN WOOD PEWEE

GREAT BLUE
HERON

BARN OWL

EGGS OF BIRDS AND REPTILES

COMMON PUFFIN

CHEWINK

GOLDEN EAGLE

ROBIN

BALTIMORE ORIOLE

CHAFFINCH

MAGPIE

RED GROUSE

SHARP-SHINNED HAWK

ALLIGATOR

IGUANA

GREEN TURTLE

FIVE-LINED SKINK

YELLOW RAT SNAKE

GECKO

BULL SNAKE

An emblem is a way of representing a person, an organization, a country or even an idea. The eagle is the emblem of the United States. The dove is the emblem of peace.

Heraldic shields, by their various colors, designs, mottos and other markings, told about the bearer's family, his rank in the world, or even some incident in his life.

In Biblical times the flag of each of the twelve tribes of Israel had an individual marking. The tribe of Judah was represented by the lion. Greek shields had individual markings, but it was the coming of knights and armor that made heraldic shields popular.

A knight's helmet hid his face. At the battle of Hastings, William the Conqueror had to take off his helmet so his men could see he was still alive. One way for armored knights to tell a friend from a foe was for them to carry heraldic shields.

Richard I was probably the first English king to carry a design on his shield. By the time of Richard III, so many designs were on shields that he started the Heraldic College in 1484.

It decided who was entitled to have a coat of arms, or design on his shield, and what it should be. Shields were distinguished by their colors, how they were divided into sections, by the symbols on them, by mottos, and other minor markings. The differences were often slight, such as a lion sitting or lying down.

Many animals, birds and even fish were used as designs on shields. They ranged from such commonly seen animals as dogs and deer to the rarely seen elephant.

The lion, considered the king of the beasts, was generally used by noblemen. But many English kings favored the leopard for their shield's heraldic device.

Legendary monsters were also used such as the griffin, a creature with the head of an eagle and body of a lion. The wyvern was a dragon-type imaginary animal with wings.

Sometimes the animal was a pun on its owner's name — a man named Bacon would have pigs on his shield, while Colfox would have fox heads on his.

Most of the terms come from the French with "gules" being French for red, "sable" meaning black and "vert," green.

Europeans were not alone in putting a coat of arms on their shields. When the Spanish conquerors in the sixteenth century invaded Mexico armed with their heraldic shields, they faced Aztec warriors whose shields also bore distinguishing designs.

32

EMBLEMS

GREAT SEAL OF THE UNITED STATES

MAPLE LEAF OF CANADA

NATIONAL EMBLEM OF MEXICO

BOY SCOUTS

OLYMPIC GAMES

GIRL SCOUTS

HERALDIC SHIELDS

BEND

BEND SINISTER

FESS

PALE

LOZENGE

SALTIRE

TRESSURE WITH FLEURS-DE-LIS

GRIFFIN RAMPANT

LION COUCHANT

VAIR

WYVERN RAMPANT

LION SEJANT

ERMINE

GULES

PURPURE

SABLE

VERT

Fish were the first animals to develop a backbone. Living in water, they use gills instead of lungs for breathing. As water filters through the gills, oxygen is allowed to reach the blood.

Most fish are covered by scales, but few statements hold true for all freshwater fish. They not only come in many shapes and sizes but display many different habits.

The lungfish can breath in water or in air, using an air bladder which acts like a lung. Because it can poke its head above the surface to get oxygen, the lungfish can survive in polluted water where other fish would die. In the dry season, as its watery home evaporates, the lungfish makes a mud cocoon about itself and lives off its body's fat. It remains there until the rains come to cover it with water.

Found in South America's great Amazon River, the 18-inch-long piranha is a vicious killer. Attacking in groups of hundreds, the piranhas can kill and reduce a cow to a mere skeleton in minutes.

Although the European eel is a freshwater fish, it will only lay its eggs far out in the ocean, swimming thousands of miles to do this. After the young are born in the ocean, they make their way to Europe where the females go far up rivers, while the males keep close to the coast. Eels can live fifty years.

The male large-mouth black bass uses its tail to scrape the stream or lake bottom until it finds a rocky spot or underwater root where the female can attach her eggs. Once she lays the eggs, he chases her away and guards the eggs until they hatch.

Even more unusual is the gaff-topsail catfish's breeding method. As the female lays the eggs, the male stores them in his mouth, not eating until they hatch almost three months later.

The beluga, a member of the sturgeon family, is probably the largest freshwater fish—almost 30 feet long and weighing nearly 3,000 pounds.

The suckerfish has no teeth. It uses its thick lips to suck in small fish and plants from the bottom of lakes and streams.

The sunfish, whose bright colors can change with changes in water temperature, is a nest builder. Once its eggs are laid in the nest, the small sunfish will bravely defend them against larger attackers.

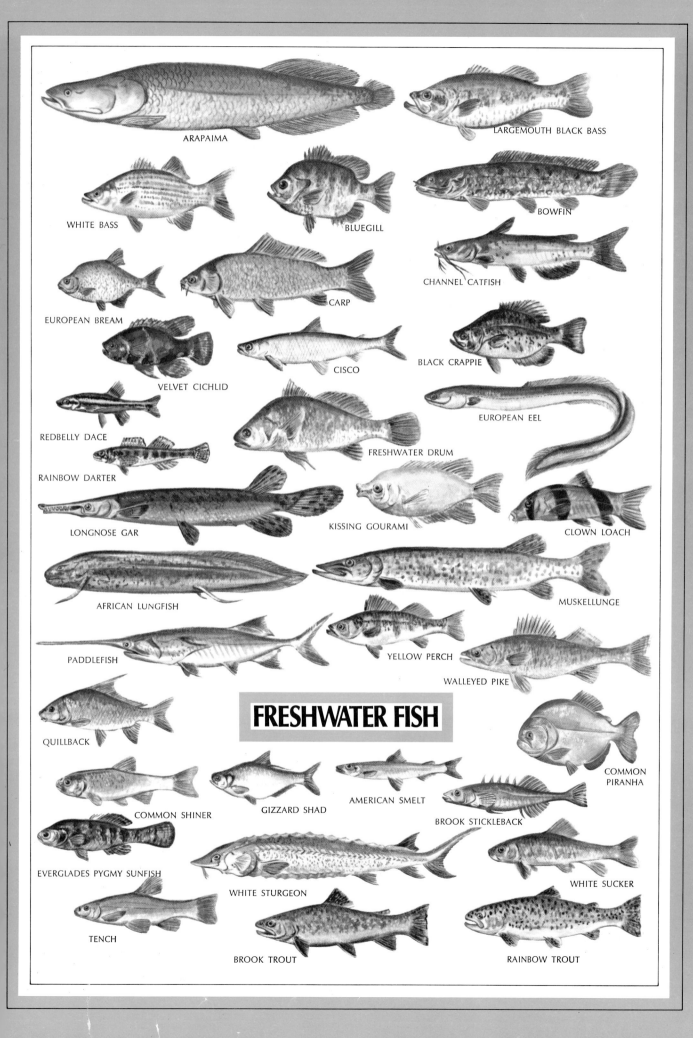

FRESHWATER FISH

ARAPAIMA

LARGEMOUTH BLACK BASS

WHITE BASS

BLUEGILL

BOWFIN

CHANNEL CATFISH

EUROPEAN BREAM

CARP

VELVET CICHLID

CISCO

BLACK CRAPPIE

REDBELLY DACE

FRESHWATER DRUM

EUROPEAN EEL

RAINBOW DARTER

LONGNOSE GAR

KISSING GOURAMI

CLOWN LOACH

AFRICAN LUNGFISH

MUSKELLUNGE

PADDLEFISH

YELLOW PERCH

WALLEYED PIKE

QUILLBACK

COMMON PIRANHA

COMMON SHINER

GIZZARD SHAD

AMERICAN SMELT

BROOK STICKLEBACK

EVERGLADES PYGMY SUNFISH

WHITE SUCKER

TENCH

WHITE STURGEON

BROOK TROUT

RAINBOW TROUT

The greatest number and variety of fish in the ocean are found in the warm waters of the tropical zone of the ocean, north and south of the equator. Many of the brilliantly colored fish live among the coral reefs.

Most ocean fish are darker on top than below. But the suckerfish, which sticks by its back to the belly of a bigger fish, is lighter colored on top than below.

Ocean fish which swim near the surface are usually colored blue on top and white below. Fish that live between 300 to 1,500 feet below the surface generally have large eyes, a silvery color and some parts of their bodies glow. From 1,500 to 6,000 feet beneath the surface fish are mostly black, have small eyes and their bodies glow in the dark depths.

Ocean fish which live near the coast or coral are normally spotted or striped to blend with the coral, rock or weeds around them.

The great barracuda found off the American coast reaches eight feet in length. It will attack a swimmer with its three-quarter-inch-long teeth.

The grouper's mouth is so large that it can swallow fish whole.

While the flying gurnard does not actually fly, it can gather enough speed before breaking above the surface to be able to glide for several yards over the water, thanks to its side fins.

The porcupine fish is a really defensive creature. It is armed with sharp spines and its front teeth have grown together, forming a pointed beak. Like the puffer, it can fill itself with water, ballooning into a big round ball which is difficult for another fish to bite into.

The Pacific sailfish is a favorite trophy of ocean fishermen, and the biggest one caught weighed over 200 pounds. Like the swordfish, to which it is related, the sailfish's upper jaw is very sharp.

The sea horse is protected by hard scales that lie partly on each other like roof shingles. This gives it a coat of armor, preventing other fish from nibbling at it. Growing to about ten inches, the sea horse's tail can circle around an object and anchor it there. After the female lays her eggs, the male becomes the "babysitter," storing the eggs in a special body patch until they hatch.

One member of the wrasse family is a swimming toothbrush. It feeds by cleaning the teeth and jaws of the larger parrot fish, which eats sticky coral animals.

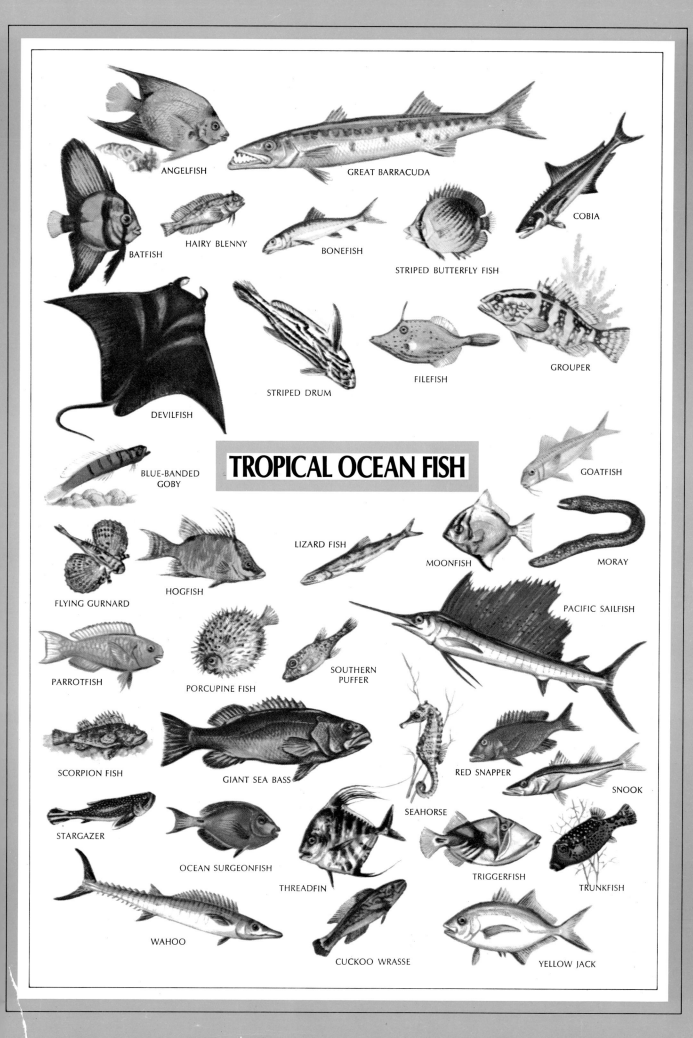

ANGELFISH

GREAT BARRACUDA

COBIA

BATFISH

HAIRY BLENNY

BONEFISH

STRIPED BUTTERFLY FISH

STRIPED DRUM

FILEFISH

GROUPER

DEVILFISH

TROPICAL OCEAN FISH

BLUE-BANDED GOBY

GOATFISH

FLYING GURNARD

HOGFISH

LIZARD FISH

MOONFISH

MORAY

PACIFIC SAILFISH

PARROTFISH

PORCUPINE FISH

SOUTHERN PUFFER

SCORPION FISH

GIANT SEA BASS

SEAHORSE

RED SNAPPER

SNOOK

STARGAZER

OCEAN SURGEONFISH

THREADFIN

TRIGGERFISH

TRUNKFISH

WAHOO

CUCKOO WRASSE

YELLOW JACK

The Egyptians were probably the first to carry something like a flag, over 4,000 years ago. At the top of a long staff they carried objects such as a fan, an emblem, a tablet with a king's name, or streamers.

Most ancient countries had flags. They were carried into battle, so the commander could see where his troops were. The flag also showed the archers the direction of the wind, so they could allow for it when they aimed their arrows.

Some North American Indians carried poles with eagle feathers attached to them.

The first flag to fly on the North American continent was a white flag with the red cross of St. George, carried by John Cabot when he landed in 1497.

State flags usually recall some event in that state's history or tell something about the state.

The color of the New Mexican state flag comes from the flag of the Spanish explorers who discovered the area. The design is an ancient Indian symbol for the sun.

The crown at the feet of Liberty on New York's flag means that Liberty will not accept the rule of any king.

The crossed red bars on the flags of Alabama and Florida come from their Confederate battle flags during the Civil War.

Ohio has the only differently shaped flag. It is in the form of a pennant. The seventeen stars recall that it was the seventeenth state to join our nation.

In 1632 King Charles I of England gave the land which now makes up the state of Maryland to Lord Baltimore. This state's flag bears the coat of arms of that English nobleman.

Louisiana's pelican suggests the state will protect its citizens just as the bird feeds her young.

California's bear flag was adopted when the American settlers there revolted against Mexican rule. The bear symbolized their determination to gain their freedom from Mexico.

Wyoming's flag shows the state seal inside the white buffalo. On that seal is the figure of a woman holding a banner that says "equal rights." In 1869, Wyoming was first to give women the right to vote, and in 1925 elected the first woman governor.

No state flag when displayed with the United States flag may be placed above it or in an equal position.

ALABAMA
 ALASKA
 ARIZONA
 ARKANSAS
 CALIFORNIA
COLORADO

CONNECTICUT
 DELAWARE
 FLORIDA
 GEORGIA
 HAWAII
 IDAHO

 ILLINOIS
 INDIANA
 IOWA
 KANSAS
 KENTUCKY
 LOUISIANA

MAINE
 MARYLAND
 MASSACHUSETTS
 MICHIGAN
 MINNESOTA
 MISSISSIPPI

 MISSOURI

STATE FLAGS

 MONTANA

NEBRASKA
 NEVADA
 NEW HAMPSHIRE
 NEW JERSEY
 NEW MEXICO
 NEW YORK

 NORTH CAROLINA
 NORTH DAKOTA
 OHIO
 OKLAHOMA
 OREGON
 PENNSYLVANIA

RHODE ISLAND
 SOUTH CAROLINA
 SOUTH DAKOTA
 TENNESSEE
 TEXAS
 UTAH

 VERMONT
 VIRGINIA
 WASHINGTON
 WEST VIRGINIA
WISCONSIN
 WYOMING

The true fly is a two-winged insect with a mouth that is used for sucking.

There are thousands of types of flies with the largest being the Australian robber fly whose wingspread is over three inches and whose body is almost two inches long.

The huge eyes of a fly are made up of many facets, which enable it to see in several directions at the same time. This is why it is so difficult to swat a fly, even when trying to strike at it from behind.

Flies can walk upside down on a ceiling, because the tiny hairs on their feet send out a sticky liquid.

Like other six-legged insects, when the fly walks it balances itself on a tripod of three legs. It walks using the front and rear legs of one side and the middle leg of the other side.

The average fly lives for about a month during the summer, but its larvae, from which the young hatch, keep alive through the winter; and the fly develops later in the warm weather.

Flies are harmful to man, animals, and plants. While the bite of the deerfly is painful and sometimes causes rabbit fever, the African tsetse fly's bite can be deadly. It gives its victim sleeping sickness.

The Hessian fly ruins wheat crops. The fruit fly damages fresh fruit.

The horse botfly is a serious threat to farm animals because its larvae feed on the animal's body tissue. After the female lays eggs in the body hair of a horse or sheep, the larvae can attack the host animal's body until they kill it.

Because it has four wings instead of just a single pair of wings, the scorpion fly is not a true fly. The dangerous-looking pincers on the male's head do not sting, but are used for holding things.

The mayfly is commonly called the shad fly. Living for only a few hours to a few days at most, mayflies do not eat and because of that generally have neither stomachs nor mouths.

Although small, the fly is a threat to man. Those flies which have blood-sucking habits spread malaria and yellow fever. Even the common housefly can pass along such major diseases as tuberculosis, dysentery, and typhoid.

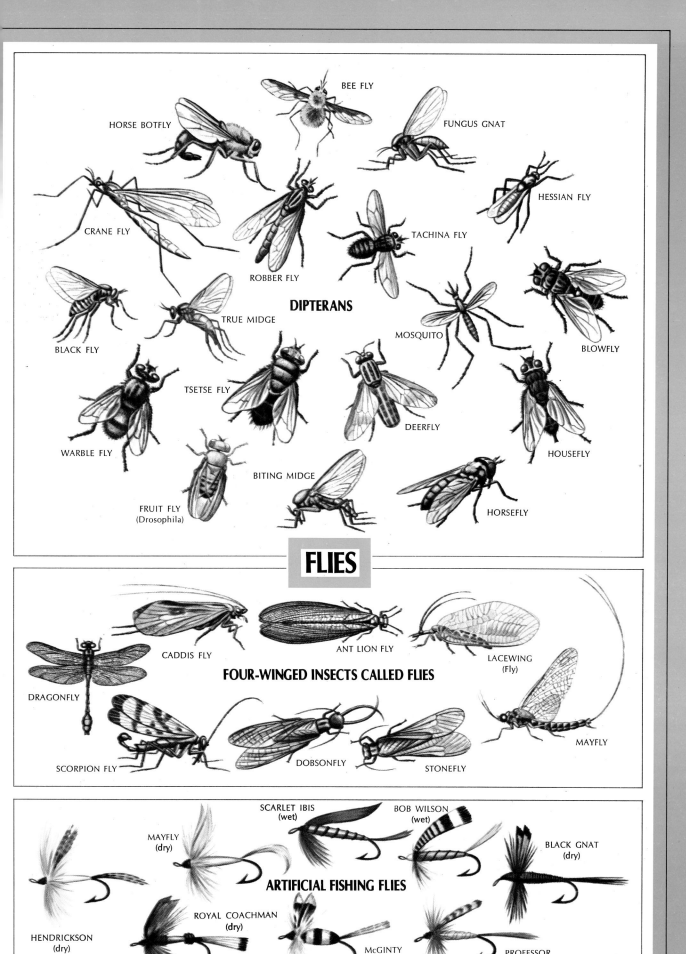

FLIES

DIPTERANS

BEE FLY

HORSE BOTFLY

FUNGUS GNAT

HESSIAN FLY

CRANE FLY

TACHINA FLY

ROBBER FLY

TRUE MIDGE

MOSQUITO

BLACK FLY

BLOWFLY

TSETSE FLY

DEERFLY

WARBLE FLY

HOUSEFLY

FRUIT FLY
(Drosophila)

BITING MIDGE

HORSEFLY

FOUR-WINGED INSECTS CALLED FLIES

CADDIS FLY

ANT LION FLY

LACEWING
(Fly)

DRAGONFLY

SCORPION FLY

DOBSONFLY

STONEFLY

MAYFLY

ARTIFICIAL FISHING FLIES

SCARLET IBIS
(wet)

BOB WILSON
(wet)

MAYFLY
(dry)

BLACK GNAT
(dry)

HENDRICKSON
(dry)

ROYAL COACHMAN
(dry)

McGINTY
(dry)

PROFESSOR
(wet)

Every state has a flower to represent it. Usually it is a flower commonly found in that state and officially named by the state legislature. But in 1891, when New York became the first to select a state flower, the school children were the ones who voted and picked the rose.

With over 37,000 varieties of American wild flowers from which to choose, four states (New York, Iowa, North Dakota and Georgia), as well as the District of Columbia, selected a member of the rose family.

Some of the state flowers chosen are hardy and can be picked without endangering them, such as the violet and goldenrod. But picking others, like the trailing arbutus and mountain laurel, endanger the plant.

The types of flowers found in the United States have changed greatly since the first colonists landed. Those that needed undisturbed cool forests have almost vanished, while others that grow best in open spaces have increased and spread.

A state flower like Massachusetts' trailing arbutus is so sensitive to changes in its surroundings that if the nearby land is used for grazing or lumber cutting, it soon dies out.

The tallest state flower is the fifty-foot-high saguaro cactus of Arizona.

While Maryland's black-eyed Susan is a native American flower, the related and more abundant common white daisy was brought to America from Europe in early times.

Our largest American orchid is a state flower, Minnesota's showy lady-slipper.

Nebraska and Kentucky have chosen goldenrod for their state flower, despite the widely held but mistaken belief that it causes hay fever. Its pollen is too sticky and wet to fly about easily.

Kansas picked one of the most dramatic-looking flowers to represent it—the sunflower, which can grow to over twelve feet high and whose flower may measure more than twelve inches across. Sunflower seeds are collected by farmers to feed their cattle and chickens.

A plant of the dry western plains, the sagebrush is typical of Nevada's dry, desert-like landscape. The wind often pulls up the tall, bushy plant and rolls it across the plains. As it rolls, the sagebrush scatters its seeds, which is why sagebrush can be seen covering miles of open ground where no other flowers grow.

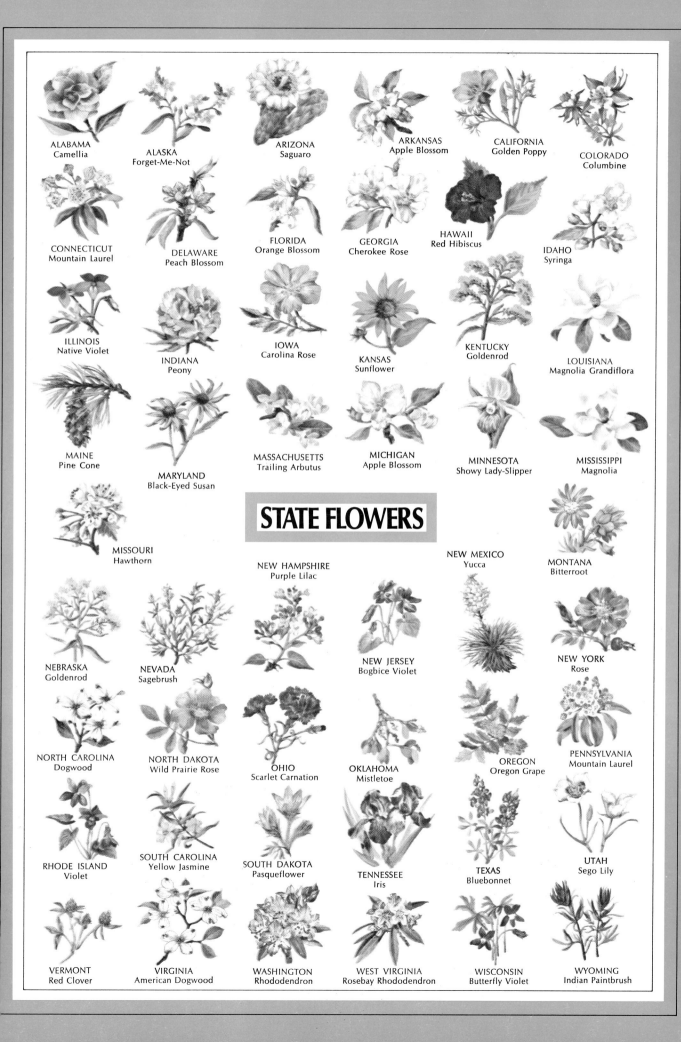

STATE FLOWERS

ALABAMA
Camellia

ALASKA
Forget-Me-Not

ARIZONA
Saguaro

ARKANSAS
Apple Blossom

CALIFORNIA
Golden Poppy

COLORADO
Columbine

CONNECTICUT
Mountain Laurel

DELAWARE
Peach Blossom

FLORIDA
Orange Blossom

GEORGIA
Cherokee Rose

HAWAII
Red Hibiscus

IDAHO
Syringa

ILLINOIS
Native Violet

INDIANA
Peony

IOWA
Carolina Rose

KANSAS
Sunflower

KENTUCKY
Goldenrod

LOUISIANA
Magnolia Grandiflora

MAINE
Pine Cone

MARYLAND
Black-Eyed Susan

MASSACHUSETTS
Trailing Arbutus

MICHIGAN
Apple Blossom

MINNESOTA
Showy Lady-Slipper

MISSISSIPPI
Magnolia

MISSOURI
Hawthorn

NEW HAMPSHIRE
Purple Lilac

NEW MEXICO
Yucca

MONTANA
Bitterroot

NEBRASKA
Goldenrod

NEVADA
Sagebrush

NEW JERSEY
Bogbice Violet

NEW YORK
Rose

NORTH CAROLINA
Dogwood

NORTH DAKOTA
Wild Prairie Rose

OHIO
Scarlet Carnation

OKLAHOMA
Mistletoe

OREGON
Oregon Grape

PENNSYLVANIA
Mountain Laurel

RHODE ISLAND
Violet

SOUTH CAROLINA
Yellow Jasmine

SOUTH DAKOTA
Pasqueflower

TENNESSEE
Iris

TEXAS
Bluebonnet

UTAH
Sego Lily

VERMONT
Red Clover

VIRGINIA
American Dogwood

WASHINGTON
Rhododendron

WEST VIRGINIA
Rosebay Rhododendron

WISCONSIN
Butterfly Violet

WYOMING
Indian Paintbrush

Over 800,000 types of insects have been named, but perhaps a million or more have yet to be found and listed.

Insects range in size from smaller than a dot to the foot-long walking stick.

All insects can be identified by their six legs and their bodies which are divided into three sections. They are cold-blooded, which is why the housefly "slows down" when the temperature drops and its blood begins to freeze.

Insects do not have a specialized nervous system like backboned animals. So when an ant's head is cut off, it may still move around for several weeks.

Some insects have two wings. Others like the dragonfly have four.

Their senses are highly developed. One male moth can follow a female's trail by her scent through the air. But insects, unlike man, cannot focus their eyes on anything which is either very close or far off. Also, they cannot close their eyes and must sleep with them open.

Many of our commonest insects have uncommon habits or abilities.

The firefly, despite its name, is a type of beetle. By a chemical action, the sides of its stomach light up, flashing light for a few seconds as it flies.

The praying mantis got its name from the way it holds its front legs when at rest. But those spiked front legs are dangerous to other insects. The praying mantis is a deadly hunter and is used by farmers to control crop-eating insects.

The locust is a type of grasshopper. Traveling in huge groups, locusts have been known to eat every green thing in their path, turning farms into barren wastelands as they go on.

The Japanese beetle was brought into the United States in the early 1900's. Since it feeds on over 250 types of plants, each year the Japanese beetle cost gardeners and farmers countless millions.

The strange but familiar buzzing sound of the cicada is made only by the male. He uses special stomach muscles and produces the sound on a drum-type membrane. The male probably makes this sound to attract female mates.

Although living in colonies like ants, termites are nearer relatives of grasshoppers and cockroaches. Since termites can digest cellulose, they can eat wood, paper and cloth.

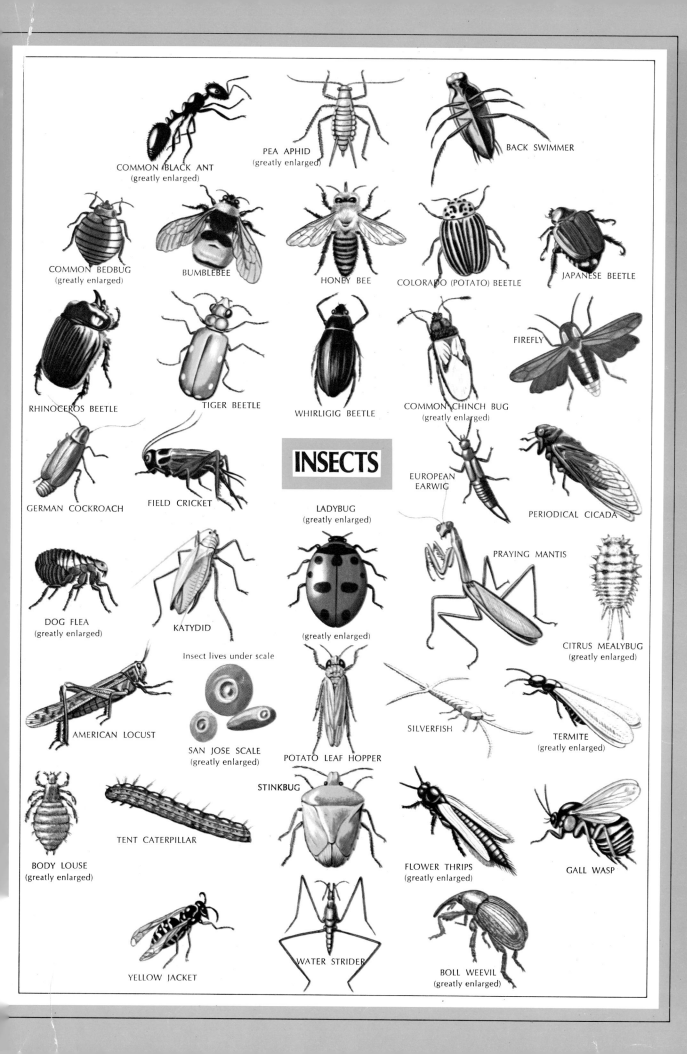

COMMON BLACK ANT
(greatly enlarged)

PEA APHID
(greatly enlarged)

BACK SWIMMER

COMMON BEDBUG
(greatly enlarged)

BUMBLEBEE

HONEY BEE

COLORADO (POTATO) BEETLE

JAPANESE BEETLE

RHINOCEROS BEETLE

TIGER BEETLE

WHIRLIGIG BEETLE

COMMON CHINCH BUG
(greatly enlarged)

FIREFLY

GERMAN COCKROACH

FIELD CRICKET

INSECTS

LADYBUG
(greatly enlarged)

EUROPEAN
EARWIG

PERIODICAL CICADA

DOG FLEA
(greatly enlarged)

KATYDID

(greatly enlarged)

PRAYING MANTIS

CITRUS MEALYBUG
(greatly enlarged)

AMERICAN LOCUST

Insect lives under scale

SAN JOSE SCALE
(greatly enlarged)

POTATO LEAF HOPPER

SILVERFISH

TERMITE
(greatly enlarged)

BODY LOUSE
(greatly enlarged)

TENT CATERPILLAR

STINKBUG

FLOWER THRIPS
(greatly enlarged)

GALL WASP

YELLOW JACKET

WATER STRIDER

BOLL WEEVIL
(greatly enlarged)

All animals which have no backbones are called invertebrates. There are some 70,000 vertebrates, or animals with backbones, while the invertebrates number about 800,000.

Invertebrates include such varied creatures as the simplest form of life, the one-celled protozoa, and the more complex, strange looking octopus.

The coquina clam is found in the south Atlantic Ocean and is also known as the butterfly shell. It gets that name because when it is washed ashore its valves, the two sides that make up a clam, are often open and still joined, looking like the wings of a butterfly.

The popular seafood mussels are found in the cooler ocean waters. Some mussels can be poisonous if they have fed on tiny sea creatures called dinoflagellates.

The octopus favors shallower water than its close relation the squid. Its foot has been changed into eight tentacles which have suction cups for helping it hold its prey. The octopus can either walk along the sea floor on its tentacles or swim by sucking water into a funnel in its body and shooting it out so that it moves like a jet-propelled plane. Most octopuses are about the size of a baseball glove, the largest being 20 feet from the tip of one tentacle to the end of the opposite tentacle.

The giant squid reaches 50 feet in length. Most squid are small sized and if chased by a big fish, they send out an inky fluid and hide in its "smoke screen."

If disturbed, the odd-looking sea cucumber throws out parts from inside its body, but it can regrow them later.

The sea slug is a shellfish without a shell. The only time it has a shell is during its embryo stage, before birth. It can take the stinging cells from some other sea animal it eats, such as the sea anemone, and use them as part of its own bodily defense.

Spiders belong to the invertebrate group. One found in the southwestern United States is dangerous. It is the scorpion. It stings with its tail, but the sting rarely kills a person. Baby scorpions are born alive, clinging to their mother's body until they are strong enough to go off on their own.

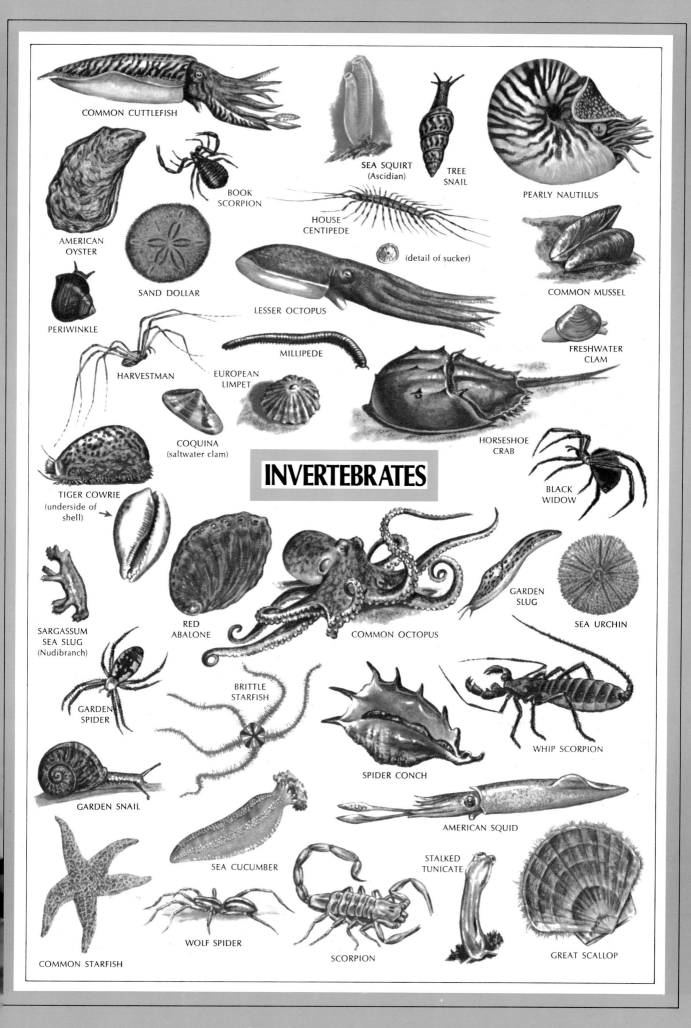

COMMON CUTTLEFISH

SEA SQUIRT
(Ascidian)

TREE
SNAIL

PEARLY NAUTILUS

BOOK
SCORPION

AMERICAN
OYSTER

HOUSE
CENTIPEDE

(detail of sucker)

COMMON MUSSEL

SAND DOLLAR

LESSER OCTOPUS

PERIWINKLE

FRESHWATER
CLAM

HARVESTMAN

EUROPEAN
LIMPET

MILLIPEDE

COQUINA
(saltwater clam)

HORSESHOE
CRAB

INVERTEBRATES

TIGER COWRIE
(underside of
shell)

BLACK
WIDOW

SARGASSUM
SEA SLUG
(Nudibranch)

RED
ABALONE

COMMON OCTOPUS

GARDEN
SLUG

SEA URCHIN

GARDEN
SPIDER

BRITTLE
STARFISH

SPIDER CONCH

WHIP SCORPION

GARDEN SNAIL

AMERICAN SQUID

COMMON STARFISH

SEA CUCUMBER

WOLF SPIDER

SCORPION

STALKED
TUNICATE

GREAT SCALLOP

Jewels are ornaments usually made from precious stones or metals.

Gems are valuable materials such as minerals and stones which have been cut and polished to be used for decorating ornaments, like scepters and crosses, or for personally worn jewelery.

Not all gems are stones. Amber comes from the hardened liquid of an ancient decayed or fossilized tree. Pearls are made by living sea creatures like the oyster. Coral is the hardened corpses of countless small sea animals.

Gems are found all over the world. The rock structure and the climate partly determine the type of gem that will be formed. The finest diamonds come from Africa. India supplies the best sapphires, while the most valuable rubies are found in Burma, and opals are native to Australia. Emeralds can be mined in such widely separated countries as Russia, Colombia, and South Africa.

The value of a gem depends on its rarity, brilliance, hardness, and color. Diamonds are generally considered the most valuable gem, because they are the hardest and most brilliant. Diamonds are used to cut sapphires and rubies, but only diamond dust can cut a diamond.

The world's largest diamond was the Cullinan, weighing one and one-third pounds. The British royal scepter has the largest cut diamond.

Four thousand years ago, the Chinese learned that striking a certain type of jade produced a musical sound. Jade carved in the shape of a fish was hung in the home to be tapped to make music. Jade was so highly valued in the Orient that poems written by the emperors were often carved on jade slates.

The agate comes in many varieties of colored bands. The bands can run parallel or in circles around each other. Most agates that are sold have been artificially colored to brighten the natural colors of their bands.

The ruby was the first gem to be made artificially on a large scale. The artificial ruby can be told from a natural one only by the difference in its interior imperfections when seen under a magnifying glass by an expert.

Long ago, gems were thought to have magical powers. Emeralds were supposed to cure blindness, while an amethyst could prevent drunkeness and opals brought bad luck.

MORGANITE

 CHRYSOPRASE

 RUBY SPINEL

 OLIVINE

 LABRADORITE

 SARDONYX

 LAPIS LAZULI

 TOURMALINE

 JASPER (Reddish, Yellow, or Brown Quartz)

 ONYX

 CITRINE

 PERIDOT

 FIRE OPAL

 RUBY

 AQUAMARINE

 BLOODSTONE

 SAPPHIRE

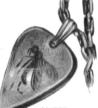 AMBER

 DIAMOND

 EMERALD

PEARL

 JADE

JEWELS AND GEMS

 MOONSTONE

 TURQUOISE

 RED CORAL

 AMAZONITE

 AGATE

 AMETHYST

 SARD

 TOPAZ

 GARNET

 KUNZITE

 ZIRCON

 ALEXANDRITE

CARNELIAN

TYPES OF CUT

 PEAR SHAPE

 AMERICAN BRILLIANT

 CABOCHON

 EMERALD CUT

 BAGUETTE

 SINGLE CUT

Lichens, liverworts and mosses were probably the first type of plants to grow on our planet.

Lichens are a hardy plant, found in many different surroundings. They grow in cold Antarctica and in the dry tropics. Some 15,000 types of lichens can be found on the ground, growing on tree stumps or bare rocks.

The lichen has two parts, an alga, which provides food, and a fungus, which stores its water.

Lichens have no flower, roots, stem or leaves.

When part of a lichen breaks off, wherever it lands, it starts growing a new lichen plant.

Some lichens, like the Iceland moss, are used to enrich bread. The reindeer moss provides that animal with food.

Mosses and liverworts belong to the same plant family. They are tiny plants which grow in crowded clusters, usually in damp places. They can reproduce in two ways. One method is from a single spore seed. The other requires the union of a male and female cell.

The tiny rootlets of mosses crack and break off pieces of rock and help form new soil. Able to hold water, they also keep the area moist so that other plants can grow.

Some mosses grow with a small capsule at the top of a long stem. At the bottom of the capsule are two layers of tiny teeth. When the moss is mature, the capsule is filled with spores, or the seeds needed to start new plants. The teeth keep the capsule closed and hold in the spores during moist weather. But when it is warm and favorable for seeding, the teeth curl back, letting the spores drop out and fly to places where they will start their life cycle.

In Lapland, the cold open regions of northern Norway, Sweden and Finland, moss is often used to line a baby's cradle.

American pioneers used moss to fill the cracks of their log cabins.

One moss has many commercial uses. The sphagnum is used in medical dressings and is also used as a fertilizer called peat moss.

The liverwort gets its strange name because people thought its tiny leaf looked like the human liver.

LICHENS

BEARD LICHEN

CRUST LICHEN

FOLIOSE LICHEN

SCALE MOSS

ICELAND MOSS

REINDEER MOSS

ROCK TRIPE

SHRUBBY LICHEN

CUDBEAR (or Archil)

LIVERWORTS

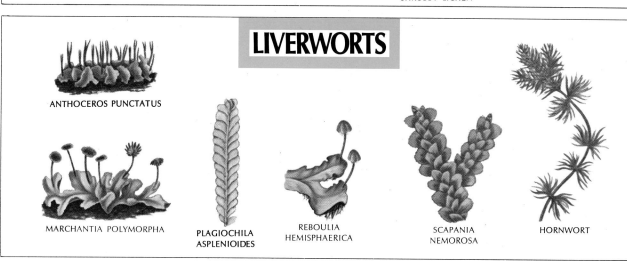

ANTHOCEROS PUNCTATUS

MARCHANTIA POLYMORPHA

PLAGIOCHILA ASPLENIOIDES

REBOULIA HEMISPHAERICA

SCAPANIA NEMOROSA

HORNWORT

MOSSES

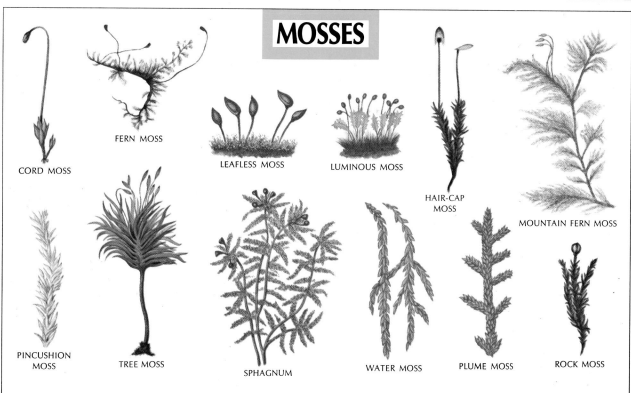

CORD MOSS

FERN MOSS

LEAFLESS MOSS

LUMINOUS MOSS

HAIR-CAP MOSS

MOUNTAIN FERN MOSS

PINCUSHION MOSS

TREE MOSS

SPHAGNUM

WATER MOSS

PLUME MOSS

ROCK MOSS

The ocean covers 70% of our world and at one point reaches a depth of about seven miles.

Where the shores of our continents are bordered by the ocean, the land usually slopes gradually out to sea. This slowly descending underwater land is called the continental shelf and reaches a depth of 600 feet. Then, it generally drops off sharply into the continental slope.

The ocean floor, like the surface of the earth, has flat plains and countless mountains.

The Mid-Atlantic Ridge is a 10,000-mile-long chain of mountains, which occasionally rise above the salty surface, forming islands like Bermuda.

Even volcanoes rise from the ocean floor. The Hawaiian Islands are volcanic islands whose bases are on the ocean bottom.

Just as we have deep canyons on land, the ocean has trenches, the deepest trench being found in the Pacific Ocean. From the surface to the bottom of the Mariana Trench it is 36,198 feet!

Between the ocean surface and its floor, countless creatures live. On the surface, microscopic animals and plants called plankton float. They are the beginning of the food chain, nourishing tiny sea creatures, who in turn serve as food for larger ones.

Beneath the ocean's surface, over 20,000 kinds of fish swim, as well as the largest sea creature of all—the 95-foot-long blue whale. This whale, which weighs 150 tons, is not a fish but a mammal, the same warm-blooded type of living creature as man.

Each type of fish maintains certain depth at which it customarily lives. A gas-filled bladder inside the fish helps it remain at its normal depth. If the fish goes too high, it may die. If it swims too deep, the increased pressure at the greater depth can crush the gas in the sack, and the fish sinks.

Plants live in the ocean as far down as sunlight can reach. But even on the dark ocean floor, sea creatures like the oyster and sea lily live.

All ocean water is salty. The Atlantic is saltier than the Pacific, and usually the ocean is less salty the deeper you descend.

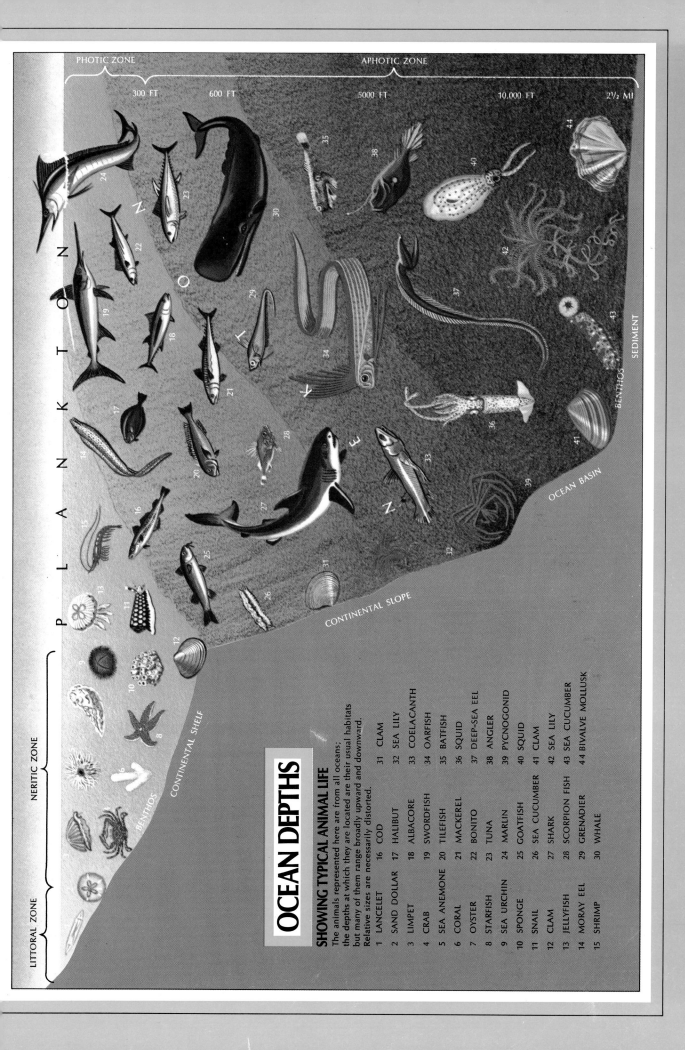

300 FT   600 FT   5000 FT   10,000 FT   2½ MI

PLANKTON

NEKTON

LITTORAL ZONE

NERITIC ZONE

BENTHOS

CONTINENTAL SHELF

CONTINENTAL SLOPE

OCEAN BASIN

BENTHOS

SEDIMENT

OCEAN DEPTHS

SHOWING TYPICAL ANIMAL LIFE

The animals represented here are from all oceans;
the depths at which they are located are their usual habitats
but many of them range broadly upward and downward.
Relative sizes are necessarily distorted.

1 LANCELET	16 COD	31 CLAM	
2 SAND DOLLAR	17 HALIBUT	32 SEA LILY	
3 LIMPET	18 ALBACORE	33 COELACANTH	
4 CRAB	19 SWORDFISH	34 OARFISH	
5 SEA ANEMONE	20 TILEFISH	35 BATFISH	
6 CORAL	21 MACKEREL	36 SQUID	
7 OYSTER	22 BONITO	37 DEEP-SEA EEL	
8 STARFISH	23 TUNA	38 ANGLER	
9 SEA URCHIN	24 MARLIN	39 PYCNOGONID	
10 SPONGE	25 GOATFISH	40 SQUID	
11 SNAIL	26 SEA CUCUMBER	41 CLAM	
12 CLAM	27 SHARK	42 SEA LILY	
13 JELLYFISH	28 SCORPION FISH	43 SEA CUCUMBER	
14 MORAY EEL	29 GRENADIER	44 BIVALVE MOLLUSK	
15 SHRIMP	30 WHALE		

Ore is a rock or mineral which has enough of some valuable element to make it worth mining or digging out of the earth.

The amount of the precious material which must be found in an ore to make mining it profitable varies greatly. There must be 30% of aluminum in an ore to make it worthwhile working, while it requires only .00005% of platinum to make its ore workable.

There are two types of ores—native and compound.

Gold, silver, platinum and copper ores are usually native, while lead, zinc, nickel and mercury are compound. A chemical change must be made to free the valuable ore from the compound.

A mineral is a non-living substance made of the same material. Except for water and mercury, minerals are all solids. Once all minerals were liquid and became solidified in various ways.

There are over 1,000 minerals, with about thirty being found in rocks. These are known as rock-forming minerals.

While often looking like rocks, minerals are composed of only one element, while rocks are usually made up of two or more minerals.

Minerals come in all colors. To find a mineral's true color you must scratch it and look at its "streak," or powder, on a piece of white paper.

Minerals vary in hardness from the softest, talc, to the hardest, diamond.

After diamond, corundum is the hardest pure mineral. It is often found in an impure form, mixed with other minerals, and that combination is called emery. Emery wheels are used for grinding and sharpening metals and emery boards are used for filing women's fingernails.

The source of most of our iron is the mineral hematite.

Pitchblende is a radioactive mineral form which we get uranium, needed to make nuclear power, and radium, used for producing x rays.

Because it resists change, heat and tarnishing, and can still be easily and delicately shaped, platinum is a valuable mineral often used as a setting for precious gems. It is also one of the heaviest substances. A pitcher filled with platinum would weigh more than twenty times as much as the same pitcher holding water.

Some minerals give off a smell when rubbed, such as pyrite. This mineral was the "fool's gold" that made many Western prospectors mistakenly think they had struck pay dirt.

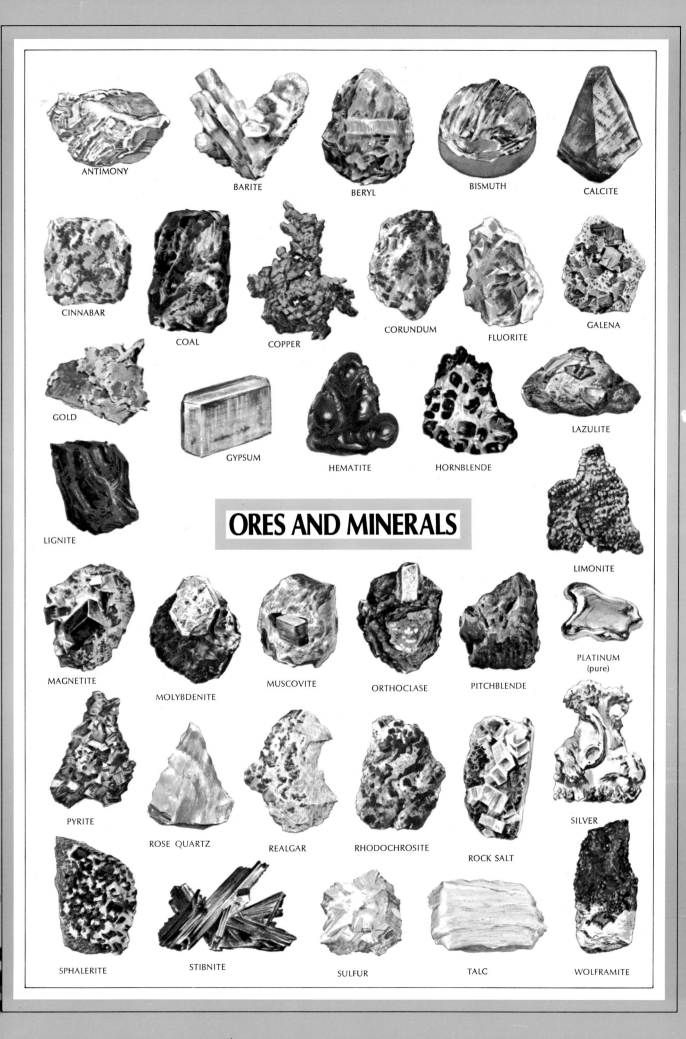

ORES AND MINERALS

Since man first began painting on the walls of his cave home, the style, or "look," of his painting has changed greatly through the centuries.

Part of this is due to the later painters seeing things differently than those artists who had painted before them. Sometimes it was due to technical changes in the material they used for paint, the surface they painted on and even the method they used to put the paint onto the surface.

At first paintings were highly realistic, almost photographs of the world around the artist at a time when the camera did not exist to give a person a lasting visual copy of what he saw. Then, as artists began leaving out details, emphasizing shadows or colors, the result became less realistic. Today, much painting is called "abstract"—it no longer represents any object.

The purpose of painting has also changed over the centuries. In the Middle Ages before printing, painting often served as an aid in teaching the viewer about an event in the Bible. Today, with most of the western world able to read and books plentiful, painting's purpose can be to explore new visual experiences, giving us a new way to see things.

Until the nineteenth century, most artists had to paint indoors due to the nature of the paint available to them. Then, when oil paint could be squeezed out of tubes, the artist moved outdoors and began studying the direct effect of natural sunlight on objects as he painted. This resulted in the style of impressionism.

In the early 1900's, there were rapid changes in painting styles with each style sharply different from previous styles.

Fauvism was an attempt by some artists to express their feelings through the use of violently brilliant colors.

Picasso was one of the founders of cubism, which broke down an object into separate parts, trying to see it all at once in terms of geometric shapes.

But whether the painting is a careful realistic portrait or the unreal figures of surrealism, whether the artist paints by adding one dot of color at a time to his pointillistic painting or swings a wet paintbrush that drips color over the canvas lying on the floor as in action paintings, the result is his individual way of seeing things and expressing what he feels, which we call his style.

ABSTRACT   Kandinsky
MME. NINA KANDINSKY

BAROQUE   Rubens   (detail)
METROPOLITAN MUSEUM OF ART

DADAISM   Duchamp
YALE UNIVERSITY ART GALLERY

FAUVISM   Matisse   (detail)
MUSÉE NATIONAL D'ART
MODERNE, PARIS

MANNERISM   El Greco
PRADO, MADRID

RENAISSANCE   da Vinci   (detail)
LOUVRE, PARIS

FUTURISM   Boccioni
GIANNI MATTIOLI, MILAN

IMPRESSIONISM   Renoir
NATIONAL GALLERY, LONDON

STYLES OF PAINTING

ABSTRACT EXPRESSIONISM
ROSE ART MUSEUM   de Kooning
BRANDEIS, UNIVERSITY

EXPRESSIONISM   Rouault
MRS. ALEX HILLMAN

REALISM   Courbet   (detail)
CITY ART GALLERY, LEEDS

ACTION PAINTING   Pollock
GIDWITZ COLLECTION

CUBISM   Picasso
PHILADELPHIA MUSEUM OF ART

NEOCLASSICISM   David   (detail)
LOUVRE, PARIS

SURREALISM   Dali
ART INSTITUTE OF CHICAGO

POSTIMPRESSIONISM   van Gogh
MUSEUM OF IMPRESSIONISM, PARIS

CHIAROSCURO   Rembrandt
TEYLERS MUSEUM, HAARLEM

POINTILLISM   Seurat
ALBRIGHT — KNOX ART GALLERY, BUFFALO

Poisonous plants are harmful to man and other living creatures, causing anything from sneezing (ragweed pollen) to itching (poison sumac) to death (pure nicotine from the tobacco plant).

Plants which cause skin irritation to people who touch them rarely trouble animals who rub against them. The irritating poison usually comes from the oily juice on their leaves. Clothes which brush against poison ivy can cause a skin rash if touched even a year later. The smoke from burning poison ivy or poison sumac can carry the irritating chemicals to someone far from the fire.

Many other plants are dangerous to man and animal if eaten. Animals are mostly the victims of such plants.

Locoweed once eaten can become habit forming for horses and cattle. They act "loco," the Spanish word meaning crazy. Cattle run about wildly and bump into things. Horses drag their legs and since they rarely eat, frequently die.

Poison from the hemlock was given to the famous ancient Greek thinker Socrates when he was sentenced to death as a result of what he taught.

The beautifully flowered and sweet smelling lily of the valley, which is used for making perfume, also produces poisonous berries.

The most dangerous type of plant to man is probably the mushroom. While many are a safe, delicious food, others if eaten can kill. The death cup has no known cure for its poison, nor is there any test, despite beliefs to the contrary, that will warn a person which mushroom is poisonous. Do not eat any wild mushroom unless someone really knows whether or not it is poisonous.

While dangerous to man and animals, many of the poisonous plants produce chemicals which are used to help man. Belladona, whose berries can cause death if eaten, is used to relax the eye muscles during an eye examination. Digitalis is vital in treating many heart diseases. Pokeweed is used in the treatment of blood diseases.

It is wise to be able to recognize those plants which are dangerous to touch, so one can avoid them, and not eat the berries or any part of a plant without checking to be sure it is not harmful.

PLANTS CAUSING SKIN IRRITATION WHEN TOUCHED

COW PARSNIP

DOG FENNEL

NETTLE

POISON IVY

POISON SUMAC

PRIMROSE

POISONOUS PLANTS

PLANTS POISONOUS WHEN EATEN   POISONOUS PART*

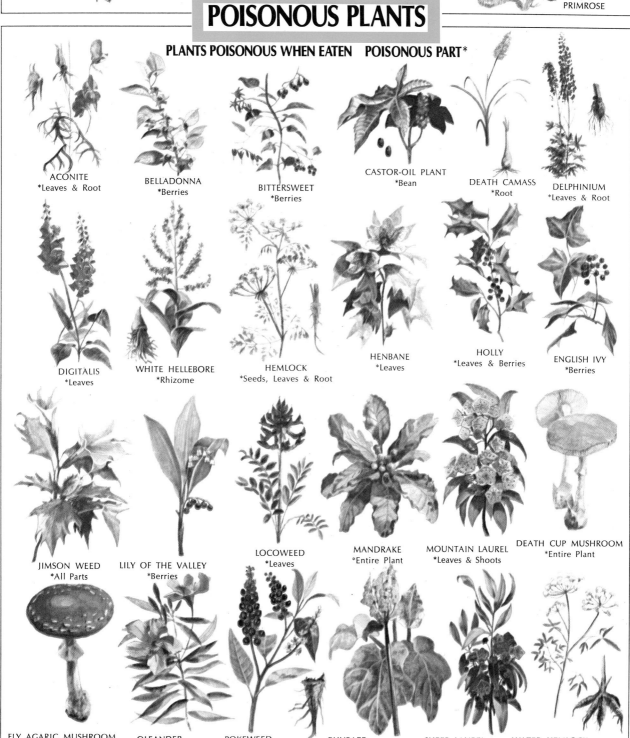

ACONITE
*Leaves & Root

BELLADONNA
*Berries

BITTERSWEET
*Berries

CASTOR-OIL PLANT
*Bean

DEATH CAMASS
*Root

DELPHINIUM
*Leaves & Root

DIGITALIS
*Leaves

WHITE HELLEBORE
*Rhizome

HEMLOCK
*Seeds, Leaves & Root

HENBANE
*Leaves

HOLLY
*Leaves & Berries

ENGLISH IVY
*Berries

JIMSON WEED
*All Parts

LILY OF THE VALLEY
*Berries

LOCOWEED
*Leaves

MANDRAKE
*Entire Plant

MOUNTAIN LAUREL
*Leaves & Shoots

DEATH CUP MUSHROOM
*Entire Plant

FLY AGARIC MUSHROOM
*Entire Plant

OLEANDER
*Leaves

POKEWEED
*Seeds & Root

RHUBARB
*Leaves

SHEEP LAUREL
*Leaves

WATER HEMLOCK
*Root

Seaweeds are a form of algae, like the green scummy covering seen on ponds.

There are thousands of types of seaweeds. Perhaps the most famous is the sargassum, a three-foot or longer brown algae, which grows in such solid masses in one part of the Atlantic Ocean that it is called the Sargasso Sea.

Brown algae reproduce either like vegetables or by a union of male and female cells, which swim out to sea from the parent seaweed.

Kelps are the great brown algae of the northern ocean waters. Anchored on the sea floor, some grow over 100 feet long, as air bladders float the plant to the surface.

Seaweeds and kelps produce many useful chemicals such as iodine, adgin, which is used to apply ink or dye to paper, and agar-agar, a gelatin substance scientists use as a base on which to grow bacteria.

Water plants live at least partly in water and are found in marshes, lakes and the sea.

The edible watercress grows and spreads so rapidly that it often chokes up streams.

The water lily's roots are held a few feet beneath the surface, while its flower floats on the water. Some water lilies bloom at night.

The roots of cattails are rich in starch and were eaten by the Russian Cossacks and later by the English who called it "Cossack asparagus."

The bladderwort is a flesh-eating plant, feeding on insects. Along its stem and leaves it has pocket-like bladders that have a mouth with a trapdoor. When an insect touches the bladder, it puffs out, sucking the insect into its mouth. Trapped inside, the insect is digested by the plant.

The most important water plant is papyrus. The ancient Egyptians wrote on it, and from preserved papyrus rolls thousands of years old, we learned much ancient history. The papyrus grows over ten feet high, but only its stem was used for making the papyrus "sheet." Stems were woven together into a "sheet," soaked in water, hammered flat and dried in the sun. About twenty sheets were pasted together and rolled into a scroll.

SEAWEEDS

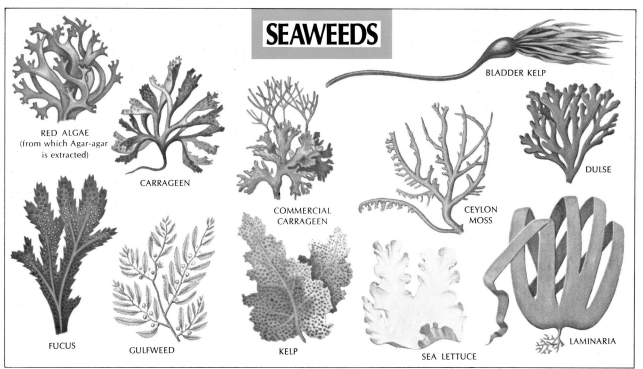

RED ALGAE
(from which Agar-agar
is extracted)

CARRAGEEN

COMMERCIAL
CARRAGEEN

BLADDER KELP

CEYLON
MOSS

DULSE

FUCUS

GULFWEED

KELP

SEA LETTUCE

LAMINARIA

OTHER WATER PLANTS

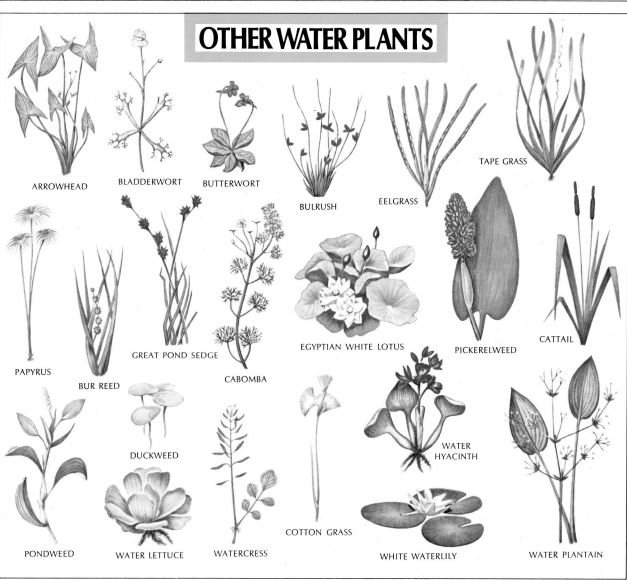

ARROWHEAD

BLADDERWORT

BUTTERWORT

BULRUSH

EELGRASS

TAPE GRASS

PAPYRUS

BUR REED

GREAT POND SEDGE

CABOMBA

EGYPTIAN WHITE LOTUS

PICKERELWEED

CATTAIL

PONDWEED

DUCKWEED

WATER LETTUCE

WATERCRESS

COTTON GRASS

WATER
HYACINTH

WHITE WATERLILY

WATER PLANTAIN

Vines and climbing plants have a stem which usually is too weak to support them. Some vines creep along the ground. Others by means of wire-like tendrils, by claspers or by sticking discs rise off the ground by holding onto another plant, a tree, a rock or a wall.

Many vines are planted for decorative purposes in gardens or on the walls of buildings, but two, the grape and hop, are used in important industries.

Cultivation of the grape vine dates back to the Biblical times of Noah. The Phoenicians probably introduced the grape into Europe about 600 B.C. The finest vines come from grapes grown where it is mild-to-hot and dry during the summer. By means of little tendrils, the grape vine climbs up and holds onto its support. A grape with not too much sugar and a lot of acid makes the best wine. If the grape has lots of sugar and not much acid, it is used to make raisins. In 1494 Columbus planted the first grape vine in the New World on the island of Haiti.

The hop is used to make beer. English hop-pickers walk on stilts so they do not have to keep moving a ladder while gathering the hops at the top of the vine.

Bittersweet, whose yellow-orange berries last through the fall, produces poisonous berries. But a liquid from its twig is made into a pain-killing medicine.

The passionflower may have been named by early missionaries in America. It reminded them of Christ's Passion. The ten petals recalled the ten Apostles present at the crucifixion. The brightly colored inner part of the flower represented the crown He wore.

The quick-growing morning glory can climb up its support to a height of over twenty feet. It owes its name to the fact that its sweet-scented flowers open in the morning and close as the sunlight gets brighter, usually being shut by noon.

In the fall, the woodbine lends its support a touch of flaming red. Once fixed to a surface by its sticky discs, a single tendril can support ten pounds.

Some vines like the Chinese yam produce roots that are eaten as food. Despite its nickname, the sweet potato is not a yam.

VINES AND CLIMBING PLANTS

BALLOON VINE

BIGNONIA

BITTERSWEET

BITTERSWEET (European vine)

BOUGAINVILLEA

CLEMATIS

CYPRESS VINE

DUTCHMAN'S-PIPE

FORSYTHIA

IVY-LEAVED GERANIUM

GOURD

FOX GRAPE

HOP

CLIMBING HYDRANGEA

BOSTON IVY

ENGLISH IVY

GROUND IVY

MATRIMONY VINE

YELLOW JASMINE

MORNING GLORY

MUSCADINE

GARDEN NASTURTIUM

PASSION-FLOWER

PERIWINKLE

POLYGONUM

SCARLET RUNNER

STRAWBERRY BUSH

SWEET PEA

TRUMPET CREEPER

TRUMPET HONEYSUCKLE

VIRGIN'S-BOWER

CHINESE WISTERIA

WOODBINE (Virginia creeper)

WOODBINE (a European honeysuckle)

CHINESE YAM

Reptiles first appeared on earth almost 200 million years ago. The 5,000 types of reptiles living today are direct descendants of those ancient ones.

Reptiles were the first animals that did not have to live in or close to the water so that their skin would keep moist.

They are cold-blooded, which means their body temperature is like the temperature around them. This is why no reptiles are found in cold climates and why many of those living in the cooler regions hibernate during winter, going underground or underwater. Most reptiles lay eggs, some bear their young alive.

The most famous group of reptiles has vanished—the dinosaurs.

There are four surviving groups:

1) Alligators and crocodiles

2) Snakes and lizards—which make up 95% of all living reptiles.

3) Tuatars—found only off the coast of New Zealand and represented by just one example.

4) Tortoises and turtles

The alligator's rounded nose distinguishes it from the crocodile with its pointed snout.

Snakes have no ear openings, but their whole bodies pick up vibrations of nearby movements. Each side of a snake's jaw moves separately, allowing it to swallow large prey. At least twice a year most snakes shed their skin. In the United States alone, there are 36 types of poisonous snakes.

The three-foot-long eastern coral snake is very poisonous. It is a highly secretive snake, living in a burrow.

Because of the pits below each eye, the copperhead is a member of the pit viper group of snakes. The pits help him find his warm-blooded prey.

When attacked, the puff adder looks very dangerous as it puffs up, hisses and strikes with its head. But it is not poisonous and rarely bites. If its threats fail, it flops over and plays dead!

There are over 2,500 types of lizards. Some can run fifteen miles an hour. One American lizard, the Gila monster, is poisonous.

Tortoises live on land. Turtles live in water and usually have webbed feet. Both are toothless, but the strong horny bill of a snapping turtle is dangerous. Some turtles like the leatherback are huge, weighing almost a ton. Turtles have been known to live over 150 years.

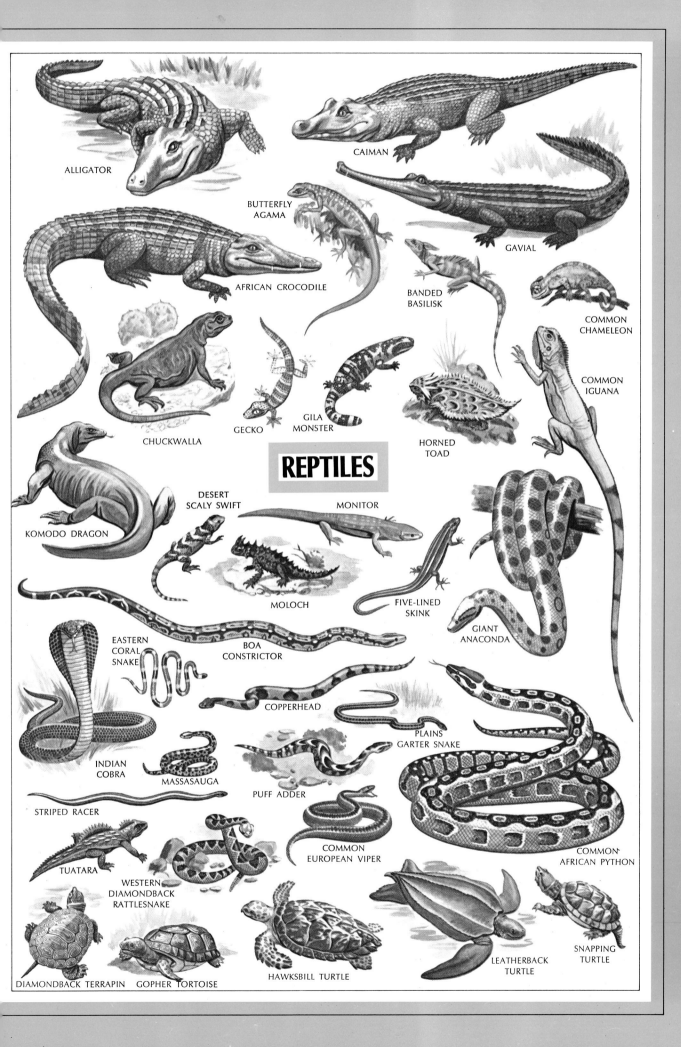

ALLIGATOR

CAIMAN

GAVIAL

BUTTERFLY AGAMA

AFRICAN CROCODILE

BANDED BASILISK

COMMON CHAMELEON

COMMON IGUANA

CHUCKWALLA

GECKO

GILA MONSTER

HORNED TOAD

REPTILES

KOMODO DRAGON

DESERT SCALY SWIFT

MONITOR

MOLOCH

FIVE-LINED SKINK

GIANT ANACONDA

EASTERN CORAL SNAKE

BOA CONSTRICTOR

COPPERHEAD

PLAINS GARTER SNAKE

INDIAN COBRA

MASSASAUGA

PUFF ADDER

STRIPED RACER

COMMON EUROPEAN VIPER

COMMON AFRICAN PYTHON

TUATARA

WESTERN DIAMONDBACK RATTLESNAKE

SNAPPING TURTLE

DIAMONDBACK TERRAPIN

GOPHER TORTOISE

HAWKSBILL TURTLE

LEATHERBACK TURTLE

A ruminant is a grazing animal that has a split hoof and eats its food in a unique and unusual way.

The ruminant swallows its food, such as grass, without chewing it. The food then enters one of its stomach's four sections, where it is temporarily stored. While the animal rests, the food is pressed into a soft mass called a cud. The cud is sent back into the animal's mouth, where it is now chewed and then reswallowed. It reenters the stomach to finally be digested.

Ruminants are found all over the world, from the low plains to the 16,000-foot-high mountain home of the Tibetan yak. Some ruminants are tame, like our cow. Others like the wild water buffalo are dangerous killers.

The bison, or buffalo as it is popularly known, gave the American Indian food, clothing and shelter. Even its droppings were used as fuel for their fires. But the white man's rifles reduced the great herds to some 541 buffalos by 1889. Today, thanks to careful protection, the buffalo is not threatened with extinction.

The soles of the Rocky Mountain goat's toes are like suction cups, helping it to climb on the narrowest ledges.

The small, three-foot-high addax is the antelope of the desert, living in North Africa and Arabia where it rarely rains. It gets its water from the desert plants it chews. Both the male and female addax have horns.

Living in the Swiss and French alps, as well as in Africa, the chamois develops a warm coat of underfur as winter approaches. Its soft skin makes the famed "shammy leather" gloves.

The okapi is a member of the giraffe family. But while the long-necked giraffe is noticeable, the okapi is so secretive that African explorers did not discover it until 1900.

By "flashing" the white pitches on its rump, a pronghorn can signal another pronghorn as far away as two miles when danger approaches. Then, they sprint off at about sixty miles an hour.

The moose is a big eater. It needs about forty pounds of food daily. Because of this, if the herd grows too numerous, many moose will starve to death in a very snowy winter.

The odd-looking gnu is an African antelope. Its even odder sounding name comes from the native Hottentot language.

The tallest animal in the world is a ruminant. It is the sixteen-foot-high giraffe, whose baby at birth is almost six feet tall.

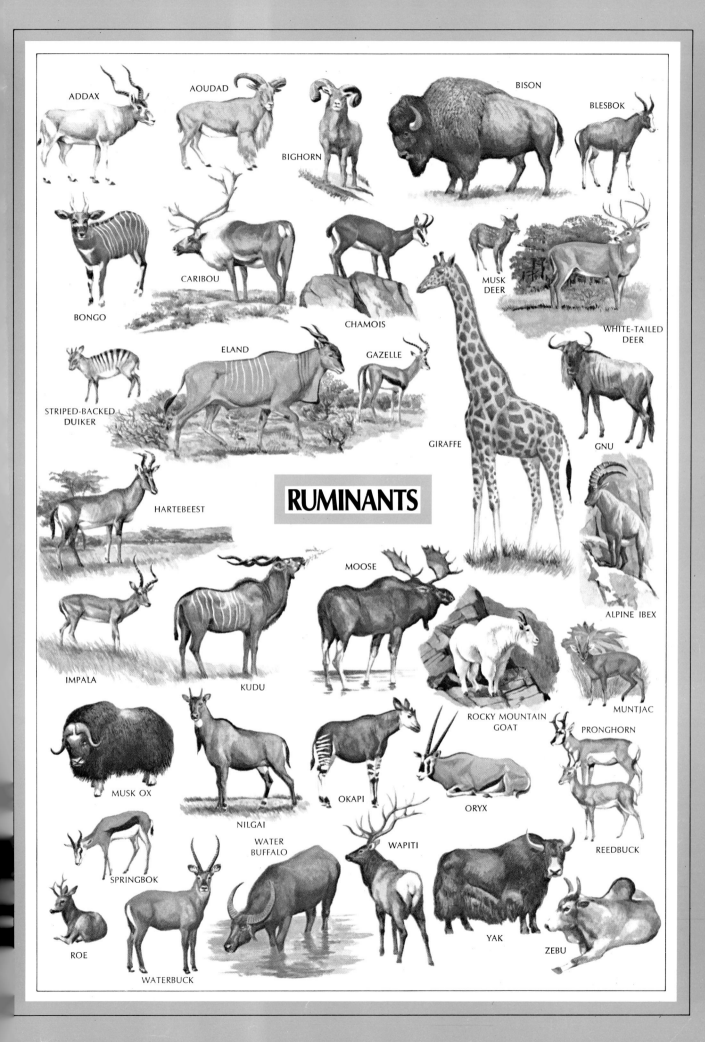

RUMINANTS

Shells are the protective hard covering formed around many types of animals found in water and on land.

Usually consisting of three layers, it is the shell's middle layer which gives off its dazzling colors. Shells continue to grow as the animal inside them ages.

They come in many forms, from the flat shell of the limpet to the two-sided shell of the oyster.

They vary in length from a tiny snail shell of less then one-tenth of an inch to the giant clam shell found in the Pacific Ocean, which is over three feet across and weighs more than 500 pounds.

Scallops favor shallow water and theirs are the common shells often washed up on our beaches.

The quahog provided the Indians not only with food but with the highly valued purple wampum made from its shell.

The gastropods, generally called sea snails, have spiral shells like the whelk. They also have a head with eyes and feelers.

Wentletraps have a staircase-like, winding type of shell. Out of the lip at the end of the shell the next and larger section is formed.

The conch is a flesh-eater, feeding on oysters and dead fish.

The barnacle's eggs after hatching swim off. Later they cling to rocks or a ship's hull. If enough barnacles stick to a ship's bottom, they can slow its speed.

Abalones probably produce the Pacific coast's most attractive large shell, measuring about twelve inches at its widest part. Highly decorative, the west coast Indians traded abalone shells with the inland tribes.

Mussels are found in the cooler ocean waters on the muddy bottom or attached to rocks or to wooden pilings. In Europe, the mussel is a very popular sea food.

The razor clam, which in one type grows to about ten inches long, is found in sandbars and sandy shallows. They live in an upright position and they feed through the top part, which sticks out of the sand. Among people who enjoy eating clams, the razor clam is said to have a delicious flavor.

Shells provide many things from buttons to the mother-of-pearl used in jewelry, from a form of money (the cowrie shells of Africa) to the American Indians' decorative wampum.

ACORN BARNACLE

SEA SNAIL (trophon)

WENTLETRAP

NAUTILUS

COQUINA

CHITON

BIVALVE (tellin)

GOLDEN COWRIE

BLUE MUSSEL

TRITON

TREE SNAIL

LIMPET

RAZOR CLAM

SHELLS

OF INVERTEBRATE ANIMALS

SCAPHOPOD

PERIWINKLE

VOLUTE

LAND SNAIL

THORNY OYSTER

SEA SNAIL

CONCH

SNAIL (sundial shell)

CALICO SCALLOP

DOG WHELK (sea snail from which purple dye is extracted)

CONE SHELL

MUREX

CROWN CONCH

WHELK

ABALONE

CHANNELED TOP SHELL (snail)

JAPANESE VOLUTE

QUAHOG

KEYHOLE LIMPET

SCALLOP (lion's paw)

OLIVE SHELL (snail)

BASKET COCKLE

Our solar system consists of the sun, our Earth and the eight other planets which go around the sun, the moons of all of the planets and some tiny planets called asteroids.

From the sun to the furthest planet, Pluto, it is approximately 3,664,000,000 miles.

While it takes our Earth one year to complete a circle around the sun, the planet closest to the sun, Mercury, goes around once every 88 days.

Planets vary in size. Jupiter is the largest. If you went from our north pole through the Earth to the south pole, it would be about 8,000 miles. From pole to pole on Jupiter, it is about 87,000 miles. That huge planet is 1,300 times larger than Earth.

Not all planets have moons. The Earth is the closest planet to the sun with a moon. Jupiter has eleven moons. One of Saturn's ten moons, Titan, is the only moon known to have some sort of atmosphere.

Because of its great size, Jupiter's "gravity," or the force that pulls things to its center, would make you weigh more than two and one-half times as much as you weigh on earth.

Saturn is the most unusual-looking planet because it has rings. Although looking almost solid when seen through a telescope, the rings are actually made up of countless tiny particles.

Over 1,500 asteroids have been listed. They are tiny, irregular-shaped planets which circle the sun between Mars and Jupiter. The largest, Ceres, is only 500 miles from pole to pole.

You can tell a planet with your naked eye because it seems to move in the sky and its light is steady, and it does not twinkle like a star. The unaided eye can see four planets in the night sky—Venus, Mars, Jupiter and Saturn.

While every school child today knows that the planets all go around the sun, only some four hundred years ago even the most learned men were positive that the sun went around the Earth.

While our planet Earth is circling around the sun in our solar system, our whole solar system—the sun and all the planets—is circling around the center of a huge galaxy, or group of stars, to which we belong. This galaxy, known as the Milky Way, contains some 100,000,000,000 stars! The Milky Way is so huge that for our solar system to make one circle around its center takes 200,000,000 years.

SOLAR SYSTEM

MEAN DISTANCE IN
MILLIONS OF MILES

PLUTO

3,700

NEPTUNE

2,800

URANUS

1,800

SATURN

887

JUPITER

484

 ASTEROIDS

ASTEROIDS

MARS

EARTH

142

VENUS

93

MERCURY

RIM OF THE SUN

67

38

Woods are divided into two large groups—softwoods and hardwoods.

A softwood tree has leaves shaped like needles, such as the pine. Except for a few trees in this group, softwoods keep their leaves all year round. Their uncovered seeds are usually carried in cones.

A hardwood tree has flat leaves, like the maple. Its leaves are shed in the fall. Their covered seeds are always held inside a seed case.

Despite their names, some softwoods are harder than hardwoods.

A tree is a plant and its wood serves two purposes. Firstly, it carries water and other food from the roots to the leaves. Secondly, it gives the plant its strength.

One of the most important qualities about wood is its strength and lightness. This is why wood is used in house building, where it serves as supporting beams for the roof.

Lumber from softwoods is used in house building, because it can take great strain. Softwoods also are used in making matches and roof shingles.

Hardwood lumber is used for making fine furniture, where its exposed grain adds to the piece's beauty. The wooden handles of most tools come from a hardwood, as do hockey sticks and baseball bats.

In the United States there are over 1,000 kinds of trees. They supply 40,000,000,000 broad feet of lumber a year.

Unlike almost every other living thing, a tree keeps growing as long as it is alive.

Growing as high as 400 feet, the redwood is the world's tallest tree. Found in California, some have been judged to have been growing for over 1,400 years!

The sitka spruce of Alaska and our west coast is possibly the most beautiful of all evergreens with its silvery foliage. Near the top it rises like a church spire.

The bark of a member of the birch tree family was used by Indians to make the light siding of their canoes.

From February to April, when the sap rises, the sugar maple is "tapped," or has its bark cut. The sap that pours out into containers is used to make maple syrup or maple sugar. One gallon of sap makes eight pounds of maple sugar.

The quacking aspen got its name because even when there seems to be no breeze its leaves move, while all the other nearby trees are motionless.

EASTERN RED CEDAR   DOUGLAS FIR   WESTERN HEMLOCK   REDWOOD

PONDEROSA PINE   SUGAR PINE   WHITE PINE   SITKA SPRUCE

SOFTWOODS

WOODS

HARDWOODS

WHITE ASH   QUAKING ASPEN   AMERICAN BASSWOOD   AMERICAN BEECH

YELLOW BIRCH   BLACK CHERRY   ROCK ELM   SWEET GUM

SHAGBARK HICKORY   SUGAR MAPLE   RED OAK   WHITE OAK

AMERICAN PLANE   TULIP TREE   BLACK WALNUT   BLACK WILLOW

Worms are a group of soft-bodied crawling animals. Some worms have long, smooth bodies, while the annelids' bodies are divided into parts, or segments.

One American ribbon worm grows to over twenty feet in length, but to see other worms you need a microscope.

What seem to be legs on the sandworm's body are bristle-like parts of its body. During the day the sandworm stays under the sand or rocks on the ocean beaches. At night it swims out in the ocean and hunts with its sharp, horny jaws.

Many worms are dangerous to man, because they are parasites, which means they live inside man's body. The tapeworm is a parasite, attaching itself inside the human intestine. It can cause serious illness. Other such worms are the hookworm, fluke and roundworm.

Once a hookworm enters a person's body through the skin, it works its way into the small intestine. It causes a victim to feel weak and look pale. Formerly a serious medical problem, today hookworm disease can be quickly cured.

Another worm, the leech, was once used to supposedly help a sick person. Before modern medicine many doctors believed that a sick patient could be cured if he lost some of his "bad blood." Once a leech attaches itself to a person's skin, it will pierce it with a bit and suck his blood. Those doctors used the medicinal leech to bleed their patients.

The earthworm is the worm commonly used as bait for fishing. It is useful to man, because as it digs through the ground, it helps bring air to the soil, making it better for growing plants and food.

The sea mouse gets its name both from its shape and the long, gray "hair" that covers its six-inch body. It lives on the sandy bottom of shallow water in the north Atlantic.

Like the earthworm, the lugworm is a digger. But instead of burrowing into garden soil, the lugworm makes its way through the sand. It grows to about eight inches.

Despite its name, the shipworm is not a worm. It is related to the clam, but its shell is very small. Shipworms enter the wooden hull of a ship or wooden dock pilings as larvae. They grow in the wood, as they use their sharp, tiny shell to hollow out a twisting, circular burrow. If you look at pieces of driftwood on the beach, you may see the holes made by shipworms.

WORMS

ANNELIDS

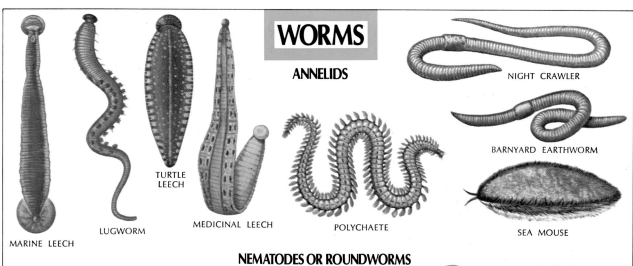

NIGHT CRAWLER

BARNYARD EARTHWORM

TURTLE LEECH

MARINE LEECH

LUGWORM

MEDICINAL LEECH

POLYCHAETE

SEA MOUSE

NEMATODES OR ROUNDWORMS

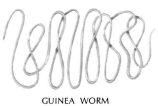
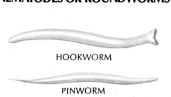

GUINEA WORM

ROUNDWORM

HOOKWORM

PINWORM

WHIPWORM

TRICHINA

NEMERTEANS OR RIBBON WORMS

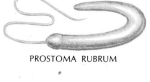

AMPHIPORUS BIMACULATUS

LINEUS LONGISSIMUS

PROSTOMA RUBRUM

PLATYHELMINTHS OR FLATWORMS

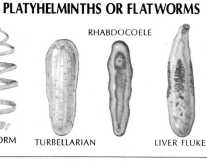
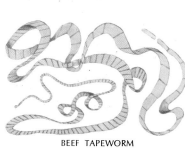

RHABDOCOELE

BLOOD FLUKE

PLANARIAN

FISH TAPEWORM

TURBELLARIAN

LIVER FLUKE

BEEF TAPEWORM

SPINY-HEADED WORM

ARROWWORM

GORDIAN WORM

PSEUDOWORMS

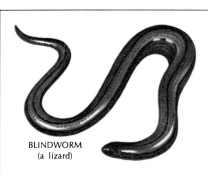
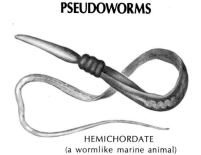

BLINDWORM
(a lizard)

HEMICHORDATE
(a wormlike marine animal)

SHIPWORM
(a mollusk)

Zoophytes are a group of animals which have no backbone, look like plants, and usually are unable to move about by their own power.

One large group of these plant-like invertebrates is the sponge. The sponge we use for washing is the cleaned skeleton of an underwater animal.

Almost all sponges live in the ocean, only a few being found in fresh water. A sponge can grow to over four feet.

One of the simplest forms of life, a sponge has no head nor any parts inside its body. Food enters the sponge through its outside pores and flows through its body.

The body, or skeleton, of sponges is made of several different types of material.

Lime sponges are the simplest of all. Between their two cell walls, they have lime "needles," which support their bodies. The grantia, an inch long, grows underwater on shells or rocks.

There are over 2,000 types of horny sponges. One, the cliona, drills tiny holes into the shell of the shellfish on which it grows.

The bath sponges include many delicate ones, and after being dried, cleaned and bleached, they are sold.

Being one of the simplest forms of life, if a sponge is broken or cut, it can generally regrow even a large missing part.

The use of sponges goes far back in history. A blacksmith washing himself with a sponge as well as tables being cleaned with sponges are mentioned in Homer's *Iliad*. Greek warriors placed sponges inside the top of their helmets to help absorb any blow, and the Romans used sponges for paintbrushes and mops. Even the New Testament tells of the use of sponges.

The Mediterranean Sea produces most commercial sponges including the hippospongia, or honeycomb sponge, whose large size, even texture and big holes makes it a popular bath sponge.

Sponge fishermen find sponges both in shallow and deep waters. Some sail a glass-bottom boat in shallow waters and when they see a cluster of sponges use a hooked pole to haul it up. In deeper water, sponge fishermen go down in diving suits to harvest these valuable animals, which once were thought to be plants.

ZOOPHYTES

SPONGES
CALCAREOUS

LEUCOSOLENIA   SCYPHA   CLATHRINA   GRANTIA

GLASS

DACTYLOCALYX   ASCONEMA

PHERONEMA   FARREA   HEXACTINELLA   EUPLECTELLA

APHROCALLISTES

SILICEOUS & HORNY

SUBERITES   HALICHONDRIA   GEODIA

SPONGILLA (freshwater)

CLIONA

TETHYA   AXINELLA   PLAKINA   HIPPOSPONGIA (common commercial species)   POTERION   MICROCIONA

CORALS

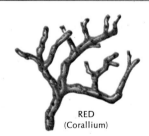
RED (Corallium)

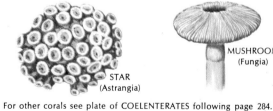
STAR (Astrangia)

MUSHROOM (Fungia)

STINGING (Millepora)

For other corals see plate of COELENTERATES following page 284.

ECTOPROCT COLONIES

TUBULIPORA (marine)

CRISTALELLA (freshwater)

PECTINATELLA (freshwater)

BUGULA (marine)